MW00714962

MASTER MIND

Thinking

Like God

Dwight J. Olney

MASTER MIND: THINKING LIKE GOD
Copyright © 2009 Dwight J. Olney

ISBN-10: 1-897373-69-4
ISBN-13: 978-1-897373-69-9

Unless otherwise indicated, all Scripture quotations are taken from the Holy Bible, New Living Translation, copyright © 1996. Used by permission of Tyndale House Publishers, Inc., Wheaton, Illinois 60189. All rights reserved.

Scriptures marked (CEV) are taken from the Contemporary English Version Copyright © 1995 by American Bible Society. Used by permission.

Scripture quotations marked (MSG) are taken from The Message. Copyright © 1993, 1994, 1995, 1996, 2000, 2001, 2002. Used by permission of NavPress Publishing Group.

Scripture quotations marked (NASB) are taken from the NEW AMERICAN STANDARD BIBLE®, Copyright © 1960, 1962, 1963, 1968, 1971, 1972, 1973, 1975, 1977, 1995 by The Lockman Foundation. Used by permission.

Scripture quotations marked (NIV) are taken from the HOLY BIBLE, NEW INTERNATIONAL VERSION®. NIV®. Copyright© 1973, 1978, 1984 by International Bible Society. Used by permission of Zondervan. All rights reserved.

Published by Word Alive Press

WORD ALIVE PRESS
Just Write!
131 Cordite Road, Winnipeg, Manitoba, R3W 1S1
www.wordalivepress.ca

Printed in Canada

Dedication

This work is dedicated to my parents, Edgar and Mabel Olney, for their tender kindness and their perpetual, sacrificial intercession before God on my behalf, and to my mother-in-law, Germaine Cadieux, for her living demonstration of the power and love of God.

Contents

Introduction

There is probably nothing that sounds more presumptuous than claiming to know the mind of God. After all, does he himself not say, *"I don't think the way you think"* (Isaiah 55:8 MSG)?

Understanding the great concepts of history, science, and technology is a challenge in itself. Comprehending the mental musings of profound thinkers like Kierkegaard or Einstein is almost impossible for the average person. How, then, can frail creatures groping around in intellectual translucence ever hope to capture the deep thoughts of the Creator? Again he says, *"For as the sky soars high above the earth, so the way I work surpasses the way you work, and the way I think is beyond the way you think"* (Isaiah 55:9 MSG).

So why write a book such as this? Is it not too lofty, let alone arrogant, to believe that we can penetrate the thinking of the Almighty, the one who holds every molecule together within the atomic structure of Mount Everest as well as the human body?

Indeed, when we check-in to this world, our thoughts and God's thoughts are light years apart. It is our natural inclination to set our minds on earthly things, to have tiny thinking. We open our eyes as newborns and see the world around us. We see earthly things. We learn naturally to think like a human. Everything in the world around us reinforces that limited, tiny thinking. *"For the world offers only a craving for physical pleasure, a craving for everything we see, and pride in our achievements and possessions"* (1 John 2:16).

All that is in the world focuses our thinking on ourselves and our selfish desires. For thousands of years, such paltry thinking has destroyed the lives of countless paupers and princes alike. The stories are well-known—from the movie star who takes her own life to end the pain of unfulfilling

Hollywood fame to the poor elderly gentleman down the street who just dies of old age, alone and unnoticed. The Bible warns us: if our thinking is limited, we are in trouble. For those who set their mind only on earthly things, *"their destiny is destruction"* (Philippians 3:19 NIV).

A radical solution is needed for this grave problem. We need a brain transplant; we need to exchange our worldly thoughts for the thoughts of God. The Bible is very clear on this matter: *"Let God transform you into a new person by changing the way you think"* (Romans 12:2). It's no wonder that the heart of God's message for humanity starts with repentance, a word which literally means 'a change of mind.' Doing it right is not so much about trying harder as about thinking differently. Right thinking leads to right living.

The Bible states a well-established fact about human behavior that very few psychologists or motivational speakers would ever challenge: *"for as he thinks within himself, so he is"* (Proverbs 23:7 NASB). It is very hard to behave differently than we think. Our lives eventually mold themselves into the shape of our thoughts.

Courageous people do not spend the majority of their days thinking fearful thoughts. Wealthy people do not acquire more assets by thinking poverty thoughts. When someone spends a good part of their day thinking about how useless they are, very little success or personal growth is likely to emerge.

Now, I concede that there is a whole theological spectrum of opinion regarding the power of positive thinking, but that is not the main issue here. The truth of the matter still remains— our thoughts have an indelible power over each of our minute daily decisions and actions, which, in turn, influences the direction of our entire lives, which consequently determines the quality of life we experience.

A good friend of mine once said, "We cannot do right until we think right. We cannot think right about anything until we think right about God." And I would add that we cannot think right about God until we start thinking like God thinks.

The good news proclaimed within this book is that it is possible to learn to think like God. Though it does not come naturally, God will reveal to us his thought patterns through a careful study of his Word and through an examination of his work in human lives. But these insights do not necessarily emerge instantly; sometimes we must scrutinize the story carefully in search of what God is actually thinking in this or that particular situation.

The thoughts presented within this work are all based on biblical narratives or a collection of passages. Sometimes, personal experiences will be used to illustrate what seems to be the point of the scriptural principal. Let me declare that all points are certainly presented with a great deal of humility.

This book in no way pretends to be exhaustive regarding the thoughts of God; such a claim would be embarrassing, certainly, and most likely blasphemous. But it does claim to offer us a chance to begin thinking some of God's thoughts about us, our lives, and our future.

Also, one thing needs to be very clear—this book is not a treatise concerning *thinking about God*, but rather, a challenge to begin *thinking like God*; there is an enormous difference between the two. Far too many theologians have spent too much time merely thinking about God. And the practice of simply thinking about God frequently results in a temporary elation of awe and wonder that passes once the television set is turned back on.

What is needed in this troubled world is not more God-thinkers but more God-thinking. There is a need for a whole host of humanity to rise up and live lives that reflect a new kind of thinking: thinking like God. When people think like God, they begin to move in harmony with their Creator, much like a married couple of forty or fifty years who act out their lives as a single entity and almost always seem to know what the other is thinking. When one moves in harmony with God, there is utter freedom and indescribable peace and joy. There is also now nothing that can truly hurt that soul.

Chapter 1

"Don't make me prove I exist."

"Only fools say in their hearts: 'There is no God.'"

~Psalm 14:1

In the beginning, God . . .
    That's how the story starts.

But how else could it have started? It is silly and almost blasphemous to ask the question: "If you were God, how would you have started the story?" That would be a human attempt to create options for God's thoughts.

There are no options for how God thinks about things. He thinks about things the way he does because he is God. *"Look now; I myself am he! There is no other god but me! I am the one who kills and gives life; I am the one who wounds and heals; no one can be rescued from my powerful hand!"* (Deuteronomy 32:39).

The revelation of God to man does not begin with a litany of arguments, hopefully trying to prove his existence to a human jury. No. It begins with a simple assumption that he is, and that he is the supreme Creator. God does not scramble to pull together a case to make his presence among us believable; he just starts talking about what he has been up to lately. There is a confidence there, not in the human sense, but still a confidence indeed.

Any other beginning to the one true story of life would taste bland and feel trivial, even embarrassing. The supreme and all-powerful Maker of Everything needs no introduction, for he himself is the source of everything. Such a notion of God's credentials needing verification smacks of the absurdity of Jeremiah's clay pots demanding explanations and answers from the potter.

God enters the room with full security and full authority, accountable to no one. When unqualified or insecure people enter a room, they do so either with an apologetic, cowering posture or with great bombastic flair, drawing attention to themselves in order to gain some control over the complex dynamics and emotions of the culture in the room that they find so threatening. Insecure humans attempt to validate and justify their worth or authority by bragging about their qualifications in both subtle and overt manners.

God enters the room with a posture that simply assumes his existence and his loving omnipotence that is purposefully directed towards establishing a home for his creation. Any other entry would be wrong, a violation of his nature and character.

There is no insecurity in God; there is no tentativeness. There is no question as to his ability or clout. He answers to no one, and no one can thwart his plans.

The purpose of this book is to help us learn to think God's thoughts so that we can operate in synergy with our Creator. And an important part of that process is differentiating between the way we think naturally as fallen humans and the way God thinks.

Human thoughts, in their natural, unredeemed state, can cause us to stumble and fall short of our goal; they will continually hinder us on our journey. I am reluctant to say they will hinder us from arriving at our destination, because learning to think like God is a process that will never end during our earthly saga. Nevertheless, along this journey we need to recognize human thoughts for what they are. We need to be able to stop ourselves and others in mid-conversation and say, "Hey, wait a minute. That is how a human thinks, not how God thinks." We must learn to see these potholes and step around them.

A human approach to the revelation of the Creator would have looked different. Instead of the short, powerful *"In the beginning, God . . ."* we would have plunged into an entire Apologetics course. We would want belief in God to be shown as rational, as pragmatic, as meeting the very needs of the creation. But while all of these things are true, they are more man-centered than God-centered—and that is bad.

By starting from an Apologetics stance, we are making two errors: we are elevating man's opinion of a matter over God's presence and we are misrepresenting God by putting him on the defensive, as if his existence truly needs to be proven before we can move forward. Even the word Apologetics—the discipline of defending the rationality of religious faith—is rooted in the notion of apologizing. "I'm sorry, but could you possibly take some time to consider these facts to see if you think they might be true?"

Please do not misunderstand me—I see the role and value of Apologetics in church history. I have, at times, been inspired and encouraged by Josh McDowell's *Evidence That Demands a Verdict* (a courtroom approach to Apologetics) and Cornelius Van Til's *In Defense of the Faith* (a philosophical approach to Apologetics), but they do not make people believe in God.

Sometimes I wonder what God thinks when he watches us scurrying around trying to come up with the perfect explanation for his existence. Is he amused by us coming to his defense? Does he think it's cute, the way we would chuckle over a little child's defense of the attributes of his dad in a playground scuffle? Or is he saddened because what used to be so obvious in times past (that God is) now requires mental gymnastics of seismic proportions to convince the skeptic? The case for Christianity will forever be promulgated by zealous advocates, but people truly believe in God when they submit their will to him, not just their intellect.

Humanity will never cease to debate the topic of God's existence, but thankfully, God will never lower himself to enter that arena. When Job, a righteous man, demanded that God show up and explain the unusual treatment he had been experiencing, God did the ultimate divine thing: he refused to answer Job's questions. He does not have to justify himself, nor should he. If God has to answer to man, he is not God. And I would even venture so far as to say if his existence begs proving, then he is not worth believing in.

Nowhere in the Scriptures does God try to prove he really exists. The Bible takes the fact of God for granted. Anyone who doubts this interpretation of God's thinking about his own existence needs to re-examine the personal name that he goes by from the earliest pages of the Old Testament—Yahweh—"I Am." The assumption, the divine confidence—it's right in his name.

Because God thinks this way about his own existence, it can be a very bad move on our part to make him prove to us that he is real. When we demand that God put on a display of validation for our satisfaction, we are treading on dangerous ground. We may likely hear the words: "I am God. Don't make me prove that I exist. You may not like the proof I give you."

Those scenarios never went well for biblical characters who took on God in a proof show.

When God began to reveal his presence and power to the Egyptians near the end of the Israelite captivity, Pharaoh hardened his heart to the Lord's command. *"And who is the Lord? Why should I listen to him and let Israel go? I don't know the Lord, and I will not let Israel go"* (Exodus 5:2). In effect, he was saying to God, "Bring it on! Prove to me that you exist." So God did bring it on; and he brought it on again, and again, until the ravished leader submitted to God's will.

But the scary part of the Exodus story is the fact that, as the plagues unveiled, God himself began to harden Pharaoh's heart so that he could not respond properly. Pharaoh first hardened his own heart to the revelation of God and his existence (Exodus 8:15, 8:19, 8:32), but then God hardened his heart (Exodus 11:10) so that he would become an even bigger spectacle of the existence of the one true God and his irresistible power (Romans 9:17). In the words of God himself, "I am doing all this *so that you may know that there is no one like Me in all the earth*" (Exodus 9:14 NASB).

Humanity demanding anything of God is terribly pretentious and presumptuous. To require that God show himself in this or that manner is downright dangerous. Whether it be the prophets of Baal at Elijah's barbeque or Ananias and Sapphira at the Acts 5 church offertory, ignoring the righteous omnipresence of God or challenging God to show himself is just plain foolish and it can cost you your life.

The psalmist rightly says, *"The wicked, in the haughtiness of his countenance, does not seek Him. All his thoughts are, 'There is no God'"* (Psalm 10:4 NASB). Every thought of the wicked is based on, and influenced by, this erroneous and dangerous presumption that everything in the universe just arrived here by fluke.

If we were to begin to think like God, we would be quick to assume his existence and think very little about trying to prove it. But now, I know what you are saying. What about honest and sincere requests for God to reveal himself? What about the wounded and hurting soul that is reaching out with all their remaining strength, sobbing, "My life so far has been an incredible and indescribable living hell; God are you really there?"

When the request for proof pours from the lips of a bowed head and a bent knee, God often graciously reveals himself to the one in need. God, in his mercy, seems to respond to the heart-cries of humble humans who ask for a sign: "God, if you really exist, reveal yourself to me."

God knows us. He knows that we are weak, that we are but dust. And he responds to broken hearts and contrite spirits who truly want to know and submit to him. But they, like everyone, must come to him in the simple faith of a child. *"And without faith it is impossible to please God, because anyone who comes to him must believe that he exists and that he rewards those who earnestly seek him"* (Hebrews 11:6 NIV).

An appropriate sign may be given; a timely miracle may arrive. But these still mean nothing without the faith component that God demands. Besides, signs and wonders can always be attributed to chance or unusual circumstance—or even the devil himself. And don't forget what Jesus said to Thomas: *"You believe because you have seen me. Blessed are those who believe without seeing me"* (John 20:29).

No matter how destitute, we cannot come to God on our terms, demanding that certain epistemological or circumstantial criteria be met. We must come to him on his terms, and that means simply believing he exists, even when our state of affairs may make us think otherwise.

The Apostle Paul tells us in his letter to the Romans that a logical and systematic examination of creation will assure us that God is real and that he is divinely powerful (1:20). But sometimes life in this fallen world is so horrid, its victims are unable to analyze anything logically or systematically. Sometimes there is more pain than anything else.

There are no easy answers. But there is a path to pursue—a transformation of the mind that leads us to think more like God. This can never be the wrong answer. Assume he exists and that he is your loving Creator. Cry out to him for faith and seek a personal revelation or confirmation from him deep within your soul. This kind of humble submission to God often generates something different than litigious proof. It generates an intangible peace that he truly is there and that he is caring for you amidst your sorrow and trauma. Do not demand, just humbly ask.

Chapter 2

"Fear me,
or fear everything else."

*"Save your fear for God, who holds your entire life—
body and soul—in his hands."*

~Matthew 10:28 MSG

For six seasons, NBC aired its highly charged "scare me/gross me out" reality show entitled *Fear Factor*. Several times I came across an episode while channel-surfing. On one such occasion, I watched a part of a show where the contestants were consuming large amounts of raw calf brains within a specified time period. It was gross. Sometimes contestants were required to eat even more disgusting animal body parts in an attempt to overcome their worst fears and win the monetary grand prize.

Whether it was eating something revolting, sliding across a cable suspended between two high office towers, or enduring thousands of cockroaches swarming all over the contestant's body and head, *Fear Factor* preyed upon our emotions and our fascination with fear in order to get us to watch the show.

It is bizarre that fear has always been a part of our entertainment—from the Roman gladiators to Hitchcock's thrillers to twenty-first century reality shows. Our fascination with playfully scaring ourselves stands in ironic contrast to the real toll fear exacts on the human race.

In its most extreme forms, fear is one of the most paralyzing of all human emotions, possessing the ability to reduce us to uninteresting, unproductive nervous wrecks. Unfettered fear has the power to hem us into a little cage, from which we are forced to timidly watch the world pass by, loathing our very existence.

Fear is Basic Humanity 101's regularly appearing uninvited guest lecturer. When we are young, we are subject to many common phobias: fear of the dark, fear of the Boogie Monster (because he lives in the dark), fear of war, fear of burglars and schoolyard bullies, fear of losing our parents, fear of being laughed at. Tragically, some children are even forced to be afraid of being abused by someone they love.

Adolescents experience their own range of fears: fear of being different and thereby socially isolated, fear of their own sexual development, fear of parental divorce, fear of crime at school, fear of academic failure, fear of choosing the right future after high school.

But fears continue to plague us through every stage of life. Once we work our way through the transitional phase of young adulthood, many of us succumb to the typical fears of grown up life: fear of not finding a mate, fear of unemployment, fear of losing investments in the stock market, fear of our kids not turning out well or being hurt by someone, fear of our kids hurting themselves as they learn to drive, fear of a scratch on our brand new BMW, fear of emotional rejection from those we love, fear of our grandchildren not being raised properly, and fear of illness or accident taking us from our family too early in life.

Even in old age, there are the common fears of insignificance, unfulfillment, being alone, being forgotten, and of course, the all-consuming title-holder: fear of death. Throughout our lives, there will always be ample opportunity for our hearts to be gripped by some form of fear.

Fear can even become a lifestyle, especially as people try to live independently of God, attempting, with inevitable futility, to control all the variables of their lives. If it goes unaddressed, fear can compound over the years. Sadly, many of the most fearful adults were once young optimists, full of hope, promise, and confidence for a good life ahead of them, their outlook having been undermined by the increasing barometer of dread they have known throughout each new decade of their lives.

But this downward spiral into a vortex of tension and concern need not be our lot. There is a better path to walk through life than one of perpetual fright. A human existence of paralyzing panic is often the byproduct of wrong thinking—purely human thinking rooted in a worldview that does not place God in his proper position of pre-eminence.

Putting God in his proper place of pre-eminence means that our primary fear should be of God himself. The Bible regularly refers to the proper path as being characterized by the fear of the Lord. So how does God think on this matter? It is quite clear: "You either choose to fear me, or you will fear everything else."

The Scriptures teach us that the fear of the Lord is the beginning of wisdom and knowledge (Proverbs 1:7, 9:10). What was Solomon talking about when he wrote these words 3,000 years ago? No one wants to be considered a fool in life. Simply stated, if you want to go the way that leads to wisdom, begin with a healthy fear of God.

Solomon wanted us to know for certain that those who fear God will win, eventually—even if they get batted around for a few innings in the process. He writes, *"Although a sinner does evil a hundred times and may lengthen his life, still I know that it will be well for those who fear God, who fear Him openly"* (Ecclesiastes 8:12 NASB).

So what is God thinking when he asks us to fear him first? What does it mean to fear God as opposed to fearing . . . stuff? Is this just referring to respect and reverence for him, or should we actually be scared of God?

Maybe.

Jesus himself said, *"Do not be afraid of those who kill the body but cannot kill the soul. Rather, be afraid of the One who can destroy both soul and body in hell"* (Matthew 10:28 NIV). These are not warm and fuzzy words: *"It is a terrifying thing to fall into the hands of the living God"* (Hebrews 10:31 NASB).

Job knew what the writer of Hebrews was talking about.

> *But he stands alone, and who can oppose him? He does whatever he pleases. He carries out his decree against me, and many such plans he still has in store. That is why I am terrified before him; when I think of all this, I fear him. God has made my heart faint; the Almighty has terrified me.* (Job 23:13–16 NIV)

Moses wanted the Israelites to get it as well: *"God, your God, is not to be trifled with—he's a consuming fire, a jealous God"* (Deuteronomy 4:24 MSG). He also wrote, *"Who understands the power of Your anger, and Your fury, according to the fear that is due You?"* (Psalm 90:11 NASB). The Psalmist expressed: *"My flesh trembles for fear of You, and I am afraid of Your judgments"* (Psalm 119:120 NASB). And again, *"You are resplendent with light . . . You alone are to be feared. Who can stand before you when you are angry?"* (Psalm 76:4, 7).

Even the Apostle Paul warned his congregation in Rome to be careful how they thought about their newly elevated spiritual position in relation to the Jews:

> *You will say then, "Branches were broken off so that I might be grafted in." Quite right, they were broken off for their unbelief, but you stand by your faith. Do not be conceited, but fear; for if God did not spare the natural branches, He will*

not spare you, either. Behold then the kindness and severity of God. (Romans 11:19–22 NASB)

Some folks have emphasized only the kindness of God. But we would do well to spend some time pondering his severity, to fear him in the most primitive understanding of the word. I don't think it's such a bad idea to be afraid of the one who hurled billions of enormous fireballs into the expanse of the heavens and now suspends them there by the word of his mouth. I don't think it's silly to fear the one who can harness the power of earthquakes, hurricanes, and volcanoes by the will of his mind. It may be quite smart to approach with trepidation and trembling the very one who holds every molecule of your brain together so that your head doesn't burst apart under the power of all the atomic energy lying therein. We must not neglect the scary parts of God. To do so is just plain dense and arrogant.

And yet the fear of God goes so far beyond just being scared of him.

The fear of God first snaps us out of our lethargy, self-centeredness, and humanistic worldly distractions. The dread of God saves us from ourselves. It is the starting point that propels us down a road to peace, purpose, and spiritual prosperity. A healthy terror of God wakes us up to reality and eternity, opens our hearts and minds to his purposes and plans, and compels us to run to his Son, who wants to be our Savior.

You see, as we truly fear God and keep his commandments, we enter into a beautiful relationship with him and the terror moves closer to reverence, which then eventually develops into sincere love. Eventually, we love God because he first loved us. And then we are able to understand verses like Proverbs 14:26–27: *"In the fear of the Lord there is strong confidence, and his children will have refuge. The fear of the Lord is a fountain of life, that one may avoid the snares of death"* (NASB).

So then it all boils down to this: to begin to think like God, we need to get this truism deep inside our heads and hearts—there are only two choices in life: we either fear God or we fear everything else.

Fearing everything else is crippling and inhibiting, while fearing God is liberating, unleashing the full potential of our body, soul, and spirit as created by the Lord.

Fear of everything else leads to a life of pitiful self-centeredness, where we nervously hoard, cower, and protect our pathetic little empires, feeling sorry for ourselves when they come crashing down. The fear of the Lord, on the other hand, leads to a life that is focused on serving and caring for others' needs in the kingdom of God. In such a world there are no deficiencies (Psalm 34:9, Proverbs 15:16).

Fear of everything else inevitably leads to an increase in sin as people chase fleeting pleasures to cover up the gnawing anxiety of their pointless existence and their impending death. The fear of the Lord empowers us to be good and kind and to love holiness while hating all that is evil (Proverbs 8:13, 16:6).

Fear of everything else can lead to uncertainty, panic, high blood pressure, and emotional chaos. The fear of the Lord brings peace and provides direction amidst confusing circumstances.

Ignoring God and fearing everything else spins its victims in a whirlwind of muddled meaninglessness, making it difficult to think straight at times. The fear of the Lord provides purpose, wisdom, and understanding. The fear of the Lord is the beginning of wisdom (Proverbs 9:10).

It's no wonder that Jesus said,

Come to me, all of you who are weary and carry heavy burdens, and I will give you rest. Take my yoke upon you. Let me teach you, because I am humble and gentle at heart, and you will find rest for your souls. For my yoke is easy to bear, and the burden I give you is light. (Matthew 11:28–30)

The fear of the Lord is a lot lighter than the fear of everything else. Which yoke will we carry for the rest of our lives—the fear of the Lord or the fear of everything else?

The words of Jesus in Luke 12:4–7 aptly sum up our discussion:

> *Dear friends, don't be afraid of those who want to kill your body; they cannot do any more to you after that. But I'll tell you whom to fear.* **Fear God**, *who has the power to kill you and then throw you into hell. Yes, he's the one to fear. What is the price of five sparrows—two copper coins? Yet God does not forget a single one of them. And the very hairs on your head are all numbered.* **So don't be afraid**; *you are more valuable to God than a whole flock of sparrows.*

Did you catch it? Fear God so that you don't have to be afraid of anything else.

Fear God, and he will take care of all that we need. He will lovingly carry us through every trial and adventure this fallen world lays before us.

Which fear is going to control our lives from this day forward? The choice is ours. To think like God means abandoning the pettiness of worldly fears and exchanging them for the blessings of the fear of the Lord.

Chapter 3

"It's going to take a little effort on your part to find me."

"When you come looking for me, you'll find me. Yes, when you get serious about finding me and want it more than anything else, I'll make sure you won't be disappointed."

~Jeremiah 29:13 MSG

It's no wonder we have warped thinking regarding finding God in the midst of our chaotic twenty-first century lives. We are not the same people we were even twenty years ago. Networking instantly with each other all over the globe is now the norm. We have become so cyber-inundated that we are tempted to think connecting with God should be as easy as clicking on a link that immediately takes us to his website. Bingo! We're there, with access to everything godly.

We don't like to wait patiently for things. It's not just our children who want instant gratification. We want our food to arrive fast, our possessions to amass steadily, our portfolios to rise quickly, and our problems to dissipate on demand. Oh, the angst when that site doesn't come up on the screen within a millisecond!

But we cannot approach God with such demanding haste. We cannot simply sign up and be good to go. He requires more than a user ID, password, and email address for future updates. Not only is there a cost to finding and following God, it takes time and effort and a will to want it more than anything else. God cannot be approached casually or half-heartedly.

My understanding of this topic was enhanced by something that happened a few years ago.

In the summer of 2004, my wife and I and our youngest daughter took a vacation to California. We had two cameras on the go and we took a lot of pictures—my wife used the print camera and I had slide film in the other. At that time we did not have a digital camera, so our old-school pictures were quite limited in number and destined for a photo album, while our slides took their place in an old fashioned slide show that used an old-fashioned slide projector.

Upon our return, I put the slides together into a meaningful presentation, set to bore family and friends alike. And when I did so, I noticed two things. One, some of my slides were pretty good. And two, some of them were not. Fortunately, I managed to capture the beauty of Monterey, Yosemite National Park, and some of the extraordinary mansions of Pacific Heights in San Francisco. A number of my shots were quite interesting, even captivating.

Occasionally, a great vacation photograph is the result of pure luck, being at the right place at the right time. Sometimes a local tips you off as to where to get a spectacular shot. Or, as is so common today, we take a whole gaggle of shots in order to get one good one. Now digital cameras instantly allow the photographer to scrutinize the quality of the pictures, but in the stone age, we had to wait days or even weeks to get our slides back. Only then could we see how many worthwhile pictures we happened to capture by fluke.

For the most part, I (and tourists in general) rarely take great photographs on a consistent basis. My picture of Alcatraz was dreary and boring, as were my images of the Golden Gate Bridge. In Los Angeles, I drove up a mountain to capture a panoramic view of the San Fernando Valley, only to get a washed out mass of grey smog. I also tried to get a shot of the famous Hollywood letters but ended up getting lost on my way there. In La Jolla, the seals in my photos of Seal Beach are so small, they could quite easily be little pieces of garbage floating in the ocean.

Why is it that tourists rarely take great photographs? What does it take to capture the ultimate beauty and majesty of a particular site? When you're on vacation and trying to take in a lot of different attractions, you are often in quite a hurry. And sometimes the weather or the lighting is not very good when you happen to be there. Tourists are seldom able to make the effort to be at the right spot at the right time to get the right angle of light in the right weather conditions.

To capture beautiful outdoor pictures, professional photographers are careful to view the scene from different angles, during different seasons, and at different times of the day. It takes a lot of planning. It takes a fair bit of effort. It can take an incredible amount of patience. Most of the time, it does not just happen. A photographer has to pursue the great shot!

Thinking about vacations and picture-taking makes me wonder—do some people fail to obtain a clear picture of the full beauty and glory of God because they have made snap judgments about him, similar to tourists quickly snapping pictures and then hustling on their way? It is common for people to make flippant judgments and improper conclusions about God based on very little evidence.

Maybe someone has a bad church experience and they think *I don't want to be a part of this. I don't want to have anything to do with a God who is running this show.* Or maybe someone has a bad encounter with a person who claims to be a Christian but is not living a stellar life. They then proceed to misjudge what the Lord is like and turn away from him, feeling disillusioned.

My photographs of the Golden Gate Bridge are a perfect illustration of what I mean. They're not very impressive because of the heavily overcast sky on the days we were there. If my pictures of the bridge were all I had ever seen of this great structure, I wouldn't think too much of it. But this is not the only encounter I have had with the Golden Gate Bridge. I have seen other wonderful pictures of it in photography books and travel brochures. I have watched its splendor in many movies, like James Bond's *A View to a Kill*. I've learned the story of its construction on an A&E television show. I know it is a spectacular suspension bridge located in a breath-taking venue at the mouth of the San Francisco Bay. I may not see that in my pictures, but I know it is true from other experiences. I wonder if some people draw conclusions about God as mistakenly as I might have looked at the Golden Gate Bridge if my own photos were my only experience of it.

The same could be said about my encounter with much of the southern California coastline during our vacation. If you were subjected to my entire vacation slide show, you would quickly realize that I have very few quality pictures of this shoreline. I know that the coast in southern California is magnificent, beautiful in every way. But almost every time we drove near it, the weather was cloudy or foggy; we could never see very much—certainly nothing worth noting. So, does my brief, disappointing, cursory experience of the southern California coastline mean that this geographical area is pathetic? Just because my own quick encounter failed to capture anything wonderful about the locale, does that mean it is useless and not worth visiting? Certainly not. Based on solid evidence provided by millions of eye-witnesses and billions of other pictures, the southern California coastline is an incredibly gorgeous sight, worthy of admiration.

The pursuit of God is quite similar to the pursuit of that perfect photograph of a scene. The quest for God involves more than just a casual observation. It involves some effort on our part, some planning, some patience, and sometimes the wise counsel or advice of others who have already gotten to know him well. Just like photographers may give each other tips about a great shot, Christians can encourage one another, especially new believers, on how to pursue the beauty and glory of God. For, without that pursuing effort, we may be in danger of missing God entirely, or certainly, missing him in all his splendor.

Three thousand years ago, when King David was old and nearing the end of his reign over the Jewish nation, he gave his son Solomon a final "pep talk for life" speech just before the young man was crowned as the new king. This exhortation is recorded in 1 Chronicles 28:1–10.

After lamenting over the fact that he, David, was not allowed to build the Temple of God because he was primarily a man of war, the old king exhorted his son to go hard for God in his lifetime. He finished up with one final refrain:

> *And Solomon, my son, learn to know the God of your ancestors intimately. Worship and serve him with your whole heart and a willing mind. For the Lord sees every heart and knows every plan and thought. If you seek him, you will find him. But if you forsake him, he will reject you forever. So take this seriously.* (1 Chronicles 28:9–10)

If you seek him, you will find him. Seeking is hard work. We all know that from our hide-and-seek days as children. We always got mad at the person who didn't take it seriously, who sat at home base and did not want to put out the necessary effort to find the others.

The writer of Psalm 119 agrees with David: *"Joyful are those who obey his laws and search for him with all their hearts"* (119:2). Four hundred years after David, the prophet Jeremiah said, *"If you look for me wholeheartedly, you will find me"* (Jeremiah 29:13).

The New Testament continues this theme. *"And without faith it is impossible to please God, because anyone who comes to him must believe that he exists and that he rewards those who earnestly seek him"* (Hebrews 11:6 NIV).

To find and know God intimately, we cannot approach him like tourists. We need to earnestly seek him at all times, with all our heart. We need to seek him when we rise out of bed in the morning. Cry out to God in the shower. Seek God as we make our way to work or school. Look for him to reveal himself in every aspect of creation around us. Get into his Word every day. Call out for him to reveal his wisdom in every situation. Beg for his way of escape when we are tempted by sin. Cling to him in the midst of our trials and disappointments. Continually pray to him with an attitude of joy and thanksgiving. Hunger for his heaven in the face of worldly distractions.

Without the necessary effort, a shallow and improper understanding of God can envelop the mind of the insipid believer. Such a poor perception of the Almighty does not properly prepare the one who truly wants to walk with the Lord. When the demands of discipleship become clarified, there will be no strength to remain faithful. Without a deep knowledge of the Holy One, we are quickly sucked back into the world's vortex when we face more than we can humanly handle.

As the rich young ruler parted ways with Jesus in the face of a call for overwhelming personal sacrifice (Mark 10), or as the majority of Jesus' disciples packed it in when the sayings got too hard (John 6), poor thinking about God—a deficit in knowledge of his character—inevitably leads to our demise when the road becomes marked with hardship and disappointment.

This fallen world is too harsh and complicated to live in with only a superficial knowledge of God. God says too many confusing things that can only be absorbed by the child of faith who can rest securely in the arms of a well-known

Creator. Do not try to shortcut your knowledge of the Lord. It will require hard work because God said so. But with that work comes the promise that the travailing saint will not be disappointed. God will meet us in our efforts.

If we seek the Lord diligently, we will get glimpses of his glory and the beauty of his majesty. Seek the Lord with all your heart and he will let you find him.

Chapter 4

"I'm good with broken stuff."

*"The sacrifice you desire is a broken spirit.
You will not reject a broken and repentant heart, O God."*

~Psalm 51:17

As humans, we are not delighted by the sight of something broken. If you have ever personally witnessed a compound fracture, you know what I mean.

In most avenues of life, when an item is broken, it implies wasted time, expense, extra work, and frustration. Broken can be annoying (zipper), painful (bone), and even disastrous (car on vacation). China shops and gift stores selling delicate wares often post warnings: "You break it, you buy it!" A broken item in a store instantly loses all its inherent value.

Learning to think like God involves a change in our outlook regarding being broken. Naturally, we want to do well. We want to succeed. We want to be strong. We want our plans to work out successfully. But what is missing in our natural thought process is a comprehension of the amazing things God can do through us when we are broken before him.

In the realm of humanity, broken often implies the end of the story; these days, we do not give much thought to repairing many of our electronic gadgets when they break. In the mind of

God, however, broken takes on a whole new meaning. When it comes to approaching God in hopes of something spectacular happening, broken is not the end of the story—it's the beginning. In fact, it's the only beginning that God is interested in, the only beginning that works.

In God's thinking, when a person is broken of their self-sufficiency and pride, then they are acceptable, fit for service, and a ready vehicle for the manifestation of divine power. Brokenness as a desired outcome is so foreign to our human minds that it requires many illustrations to understand it.

A wild stallion is a beautiful and well-proportioned animal, but as long as it is unbroken, it is useless for service. But once that horse's will has been conquered by a higher will (i.e. broken), the animal finds and enjoys the real reason for its existence.

As a carpenter, Jesus probably carved many wooden yokes for oxen. It's no wonder that he once explained salvation as *"Take my yoke upon you"* (Matthew 11:29 NASB). You see, a yoke is only for the broken and submissive.

But brokenness involves more than just a submissive heart. It involves a deep humility with an understanding of one's own sinfulness. It involves repentance, confession, restitution for wrong doing, as well as an attempt to remove opportunities for sin. Brokenness also requires a forgiving spirit and a willingness to endure wrong without retaliating. Certainly it implies honoring others above ourselves and, of course, prompt and regular obedience to the commands of God.

In sum, brokenness is the point where we powerlessly collapse before God, the point where our will gives in and we wholly depend on God. God loves when we get to this point. It is here that he can show us who he really is. It is here he can show us how good he is at dealing with broken stuff.

One of the best illustrations of this truth in the Bible is found in the story of Gideon (Judges 6–8). A careful examination of this account displays a textbook example of brokenness in the life of this unassuming Hebrew.

Historically, the Israelites had again reverted back to their evil ways, so God sent a neighboring tribe to punish them— the Midianites. On a warm autumn day, God came to Gideon while he was hiding fearfully in a wine press, thrashing grain that he hoped could be safely hidden away before their oppressors came again to steal it. The Almighty came with a message that Gideon would be the deliverer of his people.

Gideon was reluctant, being the youngest child of an insignificant family in his tribe. But God assured him, *"I will be with you. And you will destroy the Midianites as if you were fighting against one man"* (Judges 6:16). Based on that promise, Gideon moved forward and started to obey the Lord's commands.

First, he had to deal with some housecleaning issues. God told him, "If I am going to use you to save Israel, you need to trash those pagan idols on your dad's property. It's time my people understand that Yahweh is running the show, not Baal."

Gideon promptly obeyed and took ten buddies with him in the middle of the night and cut down the pagan altar, chopping it up for firewood. Then he began to summon fighters from the nearby tribes to build up his army for the inevitable Midianite confrontation. When Gideon was done recruiting, he had gathered 32,000 men. Not bad, except for the fact that those numbers still put his odds at 4:1 in favor of the Midianite team.

Those scary odds caused Gideon to clamor for signs from God to assure him that victory was coming despite being outnumbered. Through several miracles, God confirmed that Gideon was on the right track and that the Israelites would indeed be delivered.

The dialogue that came next must have been quite intriguing, perhaps sounding something like this:

Then God said, "I don't like it! I don't like the odds!"

Gideon sighed, "I knew it. I knew it all along. I knew we didn't have enough! See . . . this is what I was trying to tell you. Why else do you think I wanted all the signs?"

"No," said God. "There are too many."

"I know," said Gideon. "There's 135,000 bad guys out there!"

"Not the Midianites," replied God, "the Israelites; you've got too many Israelites."

"Too many Israelites?!?"

"Yup. When you win, those guys are going to ignore me, their God, arrogantly boasting that they did it themselves. I don't like it. Get rid of a bunch."

"Get rid of a bunch?!?"

"Yah. Tell all the scared ones to go home."

So, a perplexed and tentative Gideon proceeded to weed out his army—first the scared ones, then the ones who didn't drink properly from the stream—until there were only 300 left. Now the odds were 400:1 against Gideon, just where God wanted them to be. A humble and broken Gideon continued to do as the Lord commanded and found out that, in God's hands, some clay pots, torches, trumpets, and a little yelling could wipe out an entire massive army the size of a small city. Most of the bad guys actually killed each other off in fright.

The victory was won. The Lord had done it. Gideon had obeyed, resulting in forty years of undisturbed blessing for the Israelites while Gideon acted as their judge and the Lord was revered as their God.

In the narrative, we see that Gideon was not a perfect man, but he was a broken man—broken, yielded, and in the end, totally dependent on God to the tune of 400:1.

However, Gideon was not the only subject in this story to be broken. The children of Israel as a whole had to be broken to awaken them out of their lethargy and sin. At the beginning of the narrative, we read about their troublesome situation.

*For they (Midianites) would come up with their livestock and their tents, they would come in like locusts for number, both they and their camels were innumerable; and they came into the land to devastate it. So Israel **was brought*** *very low* *because of Midian, and the sons of Israel cried to the Lord.* (Judges 6:5–6 NASB)

Sometimes our brokenness might not be so much a choice on our part. Sometimes the Lord may need to humble us, to bring us very low to snap us out of our complacency and cause us to look up to him in order to experience his forgiveness and power.

So the nation of Israel was broken in order to start back on their road to recovery. Gideon and his army were broken and were used mightily by God. But there is one other broken thing in this story . . . the clay pots.

Judges 7:20–22 says that when the clay pots were broken and the trumpets blown, **then** *"the Lord set the sword of one against another even throughout the whole army"* (NASB). When the clay pots were broken, the light was revealed and the awesome power of God displayed. Notice the order: brokenness first, light and power second.

As so often happens in the Word of God, the Old Testament provides images or types which are fulfilled or further explained in the New Testament. In 2 Corinthians 4:5–7, we read:

You see, we don't go around preaching about ourselves. We preach that Jesus Christ is Lord, and we ourselves are your servants for Jesus' sake. For God, who said, "Let there be light in the darkness," has made this light shine in our hearts so we could know the glory of God that is seen in the face of Jesus Christ. We now have this light shining in our hearts, but we ourselves are like fragile clay jars containing this great treasure. This makes it clear that our great power is from God, not from ourselves.

What is the best way to get this light out of the clay jar? To break it.

As we continue to read this passage, we see the Apostle Paul explaining his own example of brokenness—physical persecution for being a Christian.

We are pressed on every side by troubles, but we are not crushed. We are perplexed, but not driven to despair. We are hunted down, but never abandoned by God. We get knocked down, but we are not destroyed. Through suffering, our bodies continue to share in the death of Jesus so that the life of Jesus may also be seen in our bodies. Yes, we live under constant danger of death because we serve Jesus, so that the life of Jesus will be evident in our dying bodies.
(2 Corinthians 4:8–11)

Many people of faith have experienced different kinds of hardships that have led them to a spirit of brokenness and thereby greater usefulness to God.

For some, it might be isolation. Joseph suffered fifteen long years of wrongful imprisonment after an unfair betrayal before he became tremendously useful in God's plan. He started off an arrogant teenager and emerged a humbled, powerful world leader fulfilling God's plans.

For some, it might be a mental health issue. Nebuchadnezzar was broken of pride and godlessness by seven years of mental illness until he recognized God as supreme, then repented.

For some, the pain of being sinned against might break them. David was broken as he humbly ran for his life, hiding from a jealous King Saul, learning to depend on God.

For some, it could be an accident. Joni Eareckson Tada was broken at sixteen by her diving accident. Just look at the power of God that has been manifested in that remarkable woman's life.

For some, it is physical ailment. The Apostle Paul was given a bodily illness after he received wonderful revelations from God. Paul believed this form of physical brokenness was bestowed on him to keep him from foolishly becoming proud (2 Corinthians 12:7).

Some people are broken by the consequences of their own sinful behavior. In their depravity, they submissively turn back to God. Consider the story of the prodigal son.

For others, it may be the death of a loved one. Missionary Elisabeth Elliot was broken by the tragic murder of her husband Jim in South America, and her powerful testimony over the past decades has demonstrated the beauty of a life yielded to God.

For some, it could be a business failure. How many people have been broken by financial tragedies that have driven them to their knees before the Lord, only then to find their true fulfillment, not in riches, but in God?

Of course, the physical body of Jesus was humiliated and broken on the cross so that the divine power of God could be manifested in his resurrection and his victory over sin, death, and all spiritual enemies.

How is the Lord breaking us? He wants to break us because he loves us. He wants not to destroy us but to break us and bring us under his will, where we will experience his power and purest joy.

Natural human thinking wants to resist the breaking hand of God. Natural human thinking will encourage pouting, complaining, and even challenging God in the face of being broken.

We need to know that God is good at taking care of broken things. He is breaking earthen vessels of sin, selfishness, and worldliness so that the treasure inside can come out, so that the light and power of Jesus might shine forth more brightly.

The pain and trials of this life, which might seemingly wear us down, are actually greater opportunities for God to use us mightily. We just need to learn to see it that way.

We need to learn to think differently . . . like God.

Chapter 5

"Forgiveness is my favorite part."

"But you are a God of forgiveness, gracious and merciful, slow to become angry, and rich in unfailing love."

~Nehemiah 9:17

We all know the right thing to do regarding forgiveness. We know the correct answer.

As a child, it is one of the first lessons we learn from our parents and from our teachers at school. As culprit and victim sit fearfully in the vice-principal's office, the dialogue is familiar: "Billy, what do you want to say to Tyler right now? Tyler, are you willing to forgive Billy?" Apologies and forgiveness—they are the meat and potatoes of elementary school discipline and the heart and soul of successful human relationships.

There is abundant scientific proof, both psychological and physiological, that forgiveness heals and helps us to move on in strength and peace while unforgiveness toxically debilitates our soul, draining it of all potency. In the twenty-first century, it is common knowledge that forgiveness is far more energy-efficient than unforgiveness.

Of all the unforgiveness metaphors created, perhaps the most powerful is the one that describes unforgiveness as a rotting, stinking corpse strapped to the back of the one who refuses to pardon the offender, choosing instead to nurse the pain of the wrongdoing. The filthy corpse drips its putrid juices over the one harboring the transgression, fouling every aspect of his or her character. The unforgiver pays the steep price of non-pardon, not the offender.

As we mature, we tend to develop and then exude a certain aroma of graciousness or stinginess regarding the dispensing of mercy. Old age seems to accentuate the general disposition that has been emergent throughout a lifetime of choices. Consequently, nursing homes often house a polarized population of either very happy or very sad people. Monstrously large hurdles have been miraculously overcome by words and deeds of forgiveness and mercy. Countless lives have been destroyed by lingering bitterness and unforgiveness.

But even though we all know the right answer regarding forgiveness, there may be no greater contrast between human and God-like thinking than in this vital area.

To illustrate this, consider the opening paragraphs of this chapter. Did you notice the humanly selfish tone of the argument? I myself didn't even see it until I had read it over several times.

See how the main point of forgiveness is presented from a self-help perspective? Forgive—it's good for you! Forgive—it will make you feel better! Yes, there are pleasantly powerful by-products of forgiveness that can be experienced by the one who chooses to act mercifully, but that should not be the main motivation for absolving someone of their sin against us. God does not forgive because it makes him feel better. God forgives because he is good and forgiveness is the good thing to do. As we begin to think more like God, we will forgive, not because it will make us feel good, but primarily because it is the good thing to do, yea, the only thing to do.

Even in the process of trying to write a book about the mind of God, I find myself continually slipping back into minuscule human thinking. We know we should forgive, but it is not our natural response. We are brutally harmed and we become angry and hurt. Thoughts of justice and revenge rage through our inner beings. Forgiveness is not our first response; we eventually work towards it because we know it is what we **must** do, but it is not our natural bent.

But with God, forgiveness is his favorite part. It comes naturally to him, even though he, of all people, has the right to be the most upset. He watched his creation rebel against him, disobey his commandments, and kill his son. We mock him by our independence and insolence, and yet, what does he do? He reaches out to forgive us. He can hardly wait to pardon us when we repent.

Early in the Scriptures we see this generous disposition towards mercy demonstrated to God's chosen people in the wilderness. Consider what he said to Moses regarding the construction of the Ark of the Covenant to be housed in the Tabernacle:

> *You shall put the mercy seat on top of the ark, and in the ark you shall put the testimony which I will give to you. There I will meet with you; and from above the mercy seat, from between the two cherubim which are upon the ark of the testimony, I will speak to you about all that I will give you in commandment for the sons of Israel.* (Exodus 25:21–22 NASB)

God wanted to meet his people at the mercy seat. Even as he is about to unveil his holy behavioral expectations for them, he does so in a context of forgiveness. Naturally, God is bent towards a position of mercy.

When Jesus wanted to help us understand his Father's forgiving love, he told us the story of the prodigal son (Luke 15:11–32). In this tale, because the father's forgiveness was such a joyful experience, there was even a party involved. The father did not have to work hard at mustering up the strength to forgive his errant child. Again, he could hardly wait to do it. He was watching for him every day, waiting for the opportunity to welcome him back.

By definition, prodigal means wastefully or recklessly extravagant. From a human perspective, we might rename the story "The Prodigal Father" because the love and forgiveness that he pours out on his naughty son appears to be wasteful and reckless. The lad thoroughly blew it! He cannot be trusted! He does not deserve such mercy! Is this not throwing pearls before swine? How can such a precious gift of forgiveness be wasted on such an unworthy specimen?

But that is the point of the story—the prodigal son does not deserve anything but condemnation; and yet, he receives forgiveness. God loves to forgive contemptible humans. Like I said, it's his favorite part.

While God loves to forgive, humans do it grudgingly, dutifully, and responsibly. Forgiveness is something we feel we have to work at. We don't look forward with eager anticipation to our next chance to forgive someone. Usually, we don't wake up in the morning thinking, "I hope I get a chance to forgive someone today." More likely, we are at the other end of the spectrum. We get far too much satisfaction out of rehearsing our pain and suffering and then nursing our wounds.

We want to hold on to the horrific tale of our abuse and stare at it for a while, much like we gaze in disbelief at a troubling restaurant bill, wondering how it can be so large. We want all our friends to look at the ridiculous bill too so they can share with us in wonderment and amazement at the meanness and unfairness of our plight. We are perplexed that someone could be so stupid as to act so cruelly towards us.

The prodigal son's older brother illustrates the typical human response to the sinful behavior of others. There is no natural desire to move in the direction of forgiveness. There is a disdain for the father's generosity. There is a one-sided view of justice. There is a hint of jealousy in having missed out on the "fun." The brother shows little understanding of, or appreciation for, the grace and mercy that he had been experiencing all along throughout his life.

Of course, we try to be courageously charitable. One day, when Peter was talking to Jesus, he thought he would impress the Lord with his generous spirit. *"Lord, how often should I forgive someone who sins against me? Seven times?"* Peter must have felt that his awesome kindness would astonish Jesus. *"No, not seven times,"* Jesus replied, *"but seventy times seven!"* (Matthew 18:21–22). There is no hesitation in the words of the master. There are no qualifying statements to accompany the principle. Just keep doing it as many times as they sin against you—four hundred and ninety times . . . whatever.

In this same passage, Jesus proceeded to illustrate his Father's thinking on forgiveness by telling the story of the king who wished to settle accounts with his slaves. Among the debtors was a chap who owed an insurmountable debt. The king (God) felt compassion for the poor soul (you and me) and totally forgave the debt. When that same slave refused to forgive one of his colleagues of a much smaller sum, the king was royally displeased. In fact, he was angry, and the unmerciful slave received a deposit of divine wrath upon his head.

Here we begin to wrestle with the tensions inherent within a God committed to both mercy and justice. We don't like to think of God's forgiveness as being conditional, but there are no theological calisthenics that can tone down the severity of Jesus' warning against an unforgiving heart: *"If you forgive those who sin against you, your heavenly Father will forgive you. But if you refuse to forgive others, your Father will not forgive your sins"* (Matthew 6:14–15).

I wish there was a translation that would make this sound nicer.

Those who are forgiven by God through the work of Jesus on the cross have no option but to forgive others. Comprehension of redemption, justification, propitiation, regeneration,

and sanctification requires one clear response. This is not a
superficial ritual. This is not merely about psychological or
physiological health. This is about doing the only thing that is
acceptable before God. Yes, God loves to forgive the contrite,
broken, and repentant heart, but a truly forgiven heart forgives
. . . and forgives joyfully.

Thinking like God involves a love of forgiveness that is
not natural. It may involve throwing parties, and it certainly
does not keep track—who is going to count to 490 anyway?
Undoubtedly, it involves less human effort and more
supernatural habit. But how do we get to that spectacular point
in the transformation of our thinking? How do we grow to
love forgiving?

It helps when we understand our own sinfulness and learn
to value what Jesus can create out of a redeemed life. The
sorry bloke who goes through time thinking he is clean
enough on his own to not need the cleansing that only Jesus'
blood can achieve will never fully understand the need for
forgiveness—neither his nor others'.

Going through life with an air and attitude of entitlement
will only encourage my demanding spirit. I will demand that
God fix things for me and I will insist that people pay for their
crimes. I will see my debtors as repugnant and my wounds as
spectacles worthy of self-pity. To escape this muddled thought
life, we need to change our perspective from one of entitlement to that of humility and appreciation. Seeing myself as
needy and forgiven helps me to perceive my debtors as
struggling fellow travelers and my wounds as opportunities to
show mercy.

Furthermore, we need to remember that, very often, people
do not actually know what they are doing when they are
hurting us. Jesus made that clear as he was dying on the cross:
*"Father forgive them, for they don't know what they are
doing"* (Luke 23:34). Sometimes we flatter ourselves by
concocting that great schemes have been maliciously and
clandestinely orchestrated against us, when in reality, it's just

simple decisions that have been made by people living in a fallen world. Sometimes we get hurt deeply by people who aren't thinking deeply about hurting us. It just happens. Forgive.

There is also value in remembering that *"we are not fighting against flesh-and-blood enemies, but against evil rulers and authorities of the unseen world, against mighty powers in this dark world, and against evil spirits in the heavenly places"* (Ephesians 6:12). It is easier to forgive other people when we see our earthly struggles as part of a greater spiritual struggle for righteousness and the kingdom of God.

Now, I realize that much of this chapter may sound glib to those whose life experiences include brutal sins against them and the ongoing horror that accompanies such tragic stories. But whether your story involves an alcoholic parent, a grossly abusive past, or a witness to the torture and murder of a loved one, forgiveness is never the wrong answer. It may not make the pain dissipate, but it's still the right answer.

Human thinking wants to weigh the heaviness of transgressions and mete out the appropriate punishment and bitterness. We have courts of law to respond to the human obligations of justice. But the only response that is right for the human heart is divine; it is forgiveness. When we forgive, we become more like God, and we begin to think like he thinks. And it is in that place that we are truly safe.

Chapter 6

"I'm really quite interested in radicals."

*"But I say to you, love your enemies
and pray for those who persecute you."*

~Matthew 5:44 NASB

Because God is holy, he is different from what we imagine him to be.

We cannot help but think of him as an extraordinary human—a nice old man with limitless love, unbelievable patience, and incredible wisdom. Truly he does have these attributes, but in measures far beyond measures we can ever imagine.

He is not a spectacular human; he is God and he is holy. He is pure and perfect far beyond all mortal comprehension, the exact opposite of all that is worldly. Accordingly, to think like God involves ideas and behaviors that are contrary to the ebb and flow of normal human activity. Put simply, following God involves being a radical, a rebel against worldliness. One biblical writer likened it to being an alien in someone else's country (1 Peter 2:11).

The Bible aptly sums up worldliness as the lust of the flesh, the lust of the eyes, and the boastful pride of life (1 John 2:16). To think and live naturally produces a harvest of selfish desires for physical pleasures, cravings for everything we see, and pride in our achievements and possessions. A heart and mind conformed to that of the Creator's will stand in stark contrast to the world with all its profanity.

When God instructs us to *"be holy because I . . . am holy"* (Leviticus 19:2), he is commanding us to be radical, to rebel against conforming to this world. *"Wherefore come out from among them, and be ye separate, saith the Lord, and touch not the unclean thing; and I will receive you"* (2 Corinthians 6:17 KJV). The first thought for a Christian must not be "How can I blend in more effectively?" Rather, it must be "How can I properly set myself apart from all that is worldly while still loving my neighbor as myself?" Thinking like God often has little to do with popularity amidst the establishment. Consider Jesus.

In God's economy, the worldly majority is usually wrong. *"The highway to hell is broad, and its gate is wide for the many who choose that way. But the gateway to life is very narrow and the road is difficult, and only a few ever find it"* (Matthew 7:13–14). Just ask Joshua and Caleb. God envisions his followers pushing against the flow, not drifting downstream with it.

Like father, like son. It's easy to think of Jesus as a rebel. He challenged all conventional thinking and lambasted the behavior of the religious establishment. He lived and spoke radically and called his followers to a drastic commitment. His invitation to surrender and total abandonment involved strange concepts of supernatural love for enemies, uncharacteristic peace amidst trial, deep character change, an odd sense of hope in response to tragedy, and forgiveness for terrible people.

- you need to die in order to live
- the more rights you give up, the better your life becomes

- the meek shall inherit the earth
- the first shall be last, and the last shall be first
- pray for those who persecute you

Indeed, there was nothing normative about Jesus' behavior and nothing usual about his teachings.

Jesus exemplified unselfishness, goodness, and atypical kindness; this remarkable behavior earned for him the disdain of the establishment and the adoration of outcasts. Jesus showed us what the prophet Micah's good life looks like—to do justice, love mercy, and walk humbly with your God (6:8)—but he also called people to repent of their sins. This call to a change of mind about sin, God's holiness, and mankind's need of the blood of Jesus ticked people off. His radical stance against the world and its system eventually led to his murder. And Jesus warned us that, if we are doing it right, the world will hate us just like it hates him (John 15:18). We should not take it personally.

I must admit that I struggle with this concept and with the level of hostility and negativism towards Christ. I wonder why he is universally despised and why his name is habitually profaned. Jesus Christ is wonderful. His love is beautiful. True and pure Christianity is totally attractive. If everyone in our society sincerely followed the person and teachings of Jesus Christ, there would be no crime. There would be no senseless harm and selfishness. Oh, there would still be the pain and disappointment of living in a fallen world—accidents, disasters, hurricanes, disease—but society would function ideally as a loving and cooperative unit that would seek to care for, and meet the needs of, every one of its members.

Families operating with Christian principles would function well. There would be no alcoholic fathers or controlling mothers. There would be no evil sibling meanness. The tongue would be used to bless rather than curse. Workplaces would be productive. Sporting events would be enjoyable for every participant, player, and fan. School would have more meaning.

Suicide would be non-existent and substance abuse would be an unattractive, virtually unused option. Yes, if we all truly followed Christ and embraced the good news of the gospel, life would be good. We'd never have to lock anything—car, house, or cupboard. We could trust each other implicitly in our relationships. No one would be sexually harassed or abused. No one would have to live with the painful memories of some ghastly event they experienced as a child at the hands of a selfish sinner.

Who wouldn't want to live in a society where we could all wake up every morning with a clean conscience, a pure heart, and no regrets? True Christianity is indescribably fantastic—and it's good for your health—physically, mentally, and spiritually.

Yet, why do so few people want to follow Christ? Why does his name arouse such hatred? There are several reasons for this phenomenon, but one of the most potent is Christian hypocrisy. I am convinced that Christianity has been made unattractive by the dreadful conduct of people who associate themselves with the name of Christ. Consider some of the derogatory words and phrases that have become associated with being a Christian: weirdo, hypocrite, Bible thumper, holier than thou, self-righteous, religious freak, do's and don'ts pusher, judgmental bigot. A stereotypic image has evolved: a Christian is an arrogant religious loser who can't have any fun and tries to stop everyone else from having fun too.

Well, I am a Christian and I don't want to be linked with anything on that list—and I don't think Jesus would either. But Christianity has been coupled with these evil associations because of pretend believers, who are doing something other than Christianity, and genuine believers who have demonstrated limited acumen in the execution of their Christian faith.

Some believers struggle with how to act out their radical Christian faith in a manner that is not offensive. They know they have been called to be set apart from the world, but they act unnecessarily irritating in the process. Yes, the claims of the gospel are offensive to the unrepentant heart, but our call to be radically decent people should not look radically cruel or demeaning, and certainly, not radically embarrassing. I am troubled by the level of arrogance I see in some Christian TV personalities. There is a marked difference between being confident and conceited, and there is no excuse for unprofessional behavior as we take a stand on moral issues. A rebel can still have good judgment and seasoned speech.

In an attempt to take a strong stand against evil, some Christians feel the need to rant and rave with emotional bluster and pat phrases, failing to respect the intelligence of their audience or grant the proper politeness and sensitivity to those impacted by their position. Blowing up an abortion clinic might seem like a necessary act of righteous indignation, but we probably need to leave the vengeance to God and concentrate more on delivering radical love to our neighbors.

As an exemplary Christian radical, the Apostle Paul let everyone know that he was not ashamed of Christ nor of the gospel message, and his accompanying life was a complete package that honored the Lord. He loved people powerfully, prayed for them beyond reason, and took care of his own financial needs as he preached so he would not appear to be an opportunistic freeloader. He worked diplomatically to resolve relational disputes, asked for forgiveness when he messed up, and viewed himself as the chief of sinners, totally undeserving of God's grace.

Paul's life illustrates an important point: he was a radical, but he didn't look like an idiot. This might be a simple starting point for some of us. Yes, God wants us to be radical, but not radically stupid. The message and behavior of our lives should be radically good, not radically annoying. I recognize that, even if we do things well, the world may still hate us because men love darkness more than light (John 3:19). But that should not stop us from being nice.

Christianity is radical. The plan of salvation is completely different from any other man-made religious concept. In fact, it is so far-reaching, no human could have ever created it. We are too proud. The bottom line of salvation in Christianity is that, on our own, we could never work our way up to pleasing God. His holiness and his righteousness are too fantastic; we could never string together enough good deeds to impress him and exonerate ourselves of our sin. The good news of salvation in Christ is that we don't have to try to scrape our way to God; he, in his mercy, graciously stoops down and rescues us. Because of his loving kindness, God takes the initiative and makes a way for us to be right with him. He saves us; we do not save ourselves. No matter what we have done, no matter where we have been, God is ready to implement a complete do-over, a fresh and lasting new start. This is fundamentally different than the salvation strategies resident in all man-made religions.

Now, such a generous offer might tempt us to make a cheap commitment to Christ—one quick prayer and then we'll go on our merry way, continuing to do our own thing, running our own lives. Such radical love from God deserves a better response than this. The divine plan of salvation is not just inexpensive fire insurance against an eternity in hell.

A weak commitment to Christ is not going to cut it. Think about it. The God of this universe has a plan, established before the beginning of time, to save mankind through a merciful story: the sacrifice of himself in the form of his Son. Jesus is the willing servant who strips himself of his position in heaven and reduces himself to a squirming baby, subjecting himself to the temptations and trials of human life. He completes his task with a perfect score and then dies a horrid criminal's death so that we can be cleansed . . . and then we think we can waltz into the story like strolling into a Chinese buffet to select certain items of our choice from the menu? I don't think so.

Becoming a Christian and following Christ is a radical affair. It involves our time, our money, our relationships, our emotions, our speech—everything. It involves learning to think differently, retraining our minds to counter the untruthful messages saturated therein by the media and our lackluster upbringings. Most of all, it involves a thorough surrender to the lordship of Jesus Christ and a sweeping lifestyle change that other people notice.

Somewhere along the line, a mistaken perception has formed—that Christianity is just a whack of rules. Jesus Christ is not interested in turning us into a bunch of little well-behaved citizens. No, it is far more radical than that. Jesus did not die on the cross in order to make us a little army of goody-goody robots. He died on the cross to buy back a lost humanity and to bring us into a friendly relationship with God. He died on the cross and rose from the dead in order to radically change us, not just on the outside, but a change that permeates right through our inner being. We can obey all the rules in the world and still be dirty on the inside. Jesus died for us that we may become new creations, clean inside and out and radically different from what we would be without him.

But a radical commitment to Christ is not about being perfect. No, it's about going God's way and being willing to sustain a radical faith amidst hardship and trial. It's about continually resisting the influence that the world dumps on our souls. It's about rebelling against everything that the devil schemes for us.

Look at the Apostle Peter, for example. He loved Jesus with all his heart and he passionately followed him; he was even ready to die for him. Yet this boisterous and friendly radical made plenty of blunders along the way and Jesus continued to extend him grace. We, like Peter, will continue to flounder, but we must never forget—no matter how imperfect it may look at times—a radical commitment to Christ is the only one that counts. Truly, God is interested in radicals.

Chapter 7

"Here's what I mean by faith."

"By faith these people overthrew kingdoms . . .
but others were tortured."

~Hebrews 11:33-35

In 1987, George Michael's *Faith* skyrocketed to #1 on the Billboard Hot 100 hits and the US R&B charts. In his wildly successful hit single, the British songwriter rids himself of a substandard girlfriend (*I'm showing you the door*) because of her emotional abuse (*Time to pick my heart up off the floor*). As he wrestles with the angst of his decision, he concludes:

Well I need someone to hold me
But I'll wait for something more

Yes I've gotta have faith...[1]

George Michael's lyrics sum up the human perspective of faith: wishful thinking, a hope or belief that circumstances will work out or that life will improve. Or, in his case, that truly

---

[1] George Michael, *Faith* © 1985 Big Geoff Overseas Ltd and Morrison Leahy Music Ltd (Warner/Chappell Music Ltd in USA).

there is a better girl out there for him than what he has been tolerating lately.

When God thinks about faith, the concept is a little deeper and a little more complex than what is portrayed in popular culture and promulgated by typical human behavior. Faith in God is a confidence in his goodness, his sovereignty, and his Word. It is a calm, steady belief that God is enough to meet all our needs and that, no matter what we experience, he is good and he is working things out for our good because he loves us.

There are so many things that could be said about faith, but the simplest way to gain insight into the mind of God on this subject is to observe what he says about it in the eleventh and twelfth chapters of the book of Hebrews.

The first observation from this passage is that faith pleases God. *"For by it, men of old gained approval"* (Hebrews 11:2 NASB).

God is not only our Creator, he is our heavenly Father. As a parent, I know the pleasure of having children who trust me and have confidence in my ability to take care of them. When I made tough but necessary decisions on behalf of my young children, I was delighted when they accepted the verdict and had faith in me as their loving father. Their faith in me pleased me.

Our faith in God also brings him pleasure, but in God's case, this disposition of trust is an absolute requirement; it is not an optional matter. Hebrews 11:6 says, *"without faith it is impossible to please God"* (NIV). We cannot please him any other way, plain and simple.

So when we trust him fully, what outcome can we expect? What else can we observe from this passage? Hebrews 11 also clearly tells us that faith in God sometimes changes our circumstances. Sometimes we find ourselves in a tough situation and our faith in God brings about a happy resolution to our troubled story. The bulk of the chapter is packed full of detailed illustrations of this fact:

- By faith, Abel was declared righteous because of his obedient sacrifice.

- By faith, Enoch was taken up to be with God without dying.

- By faith, Noah received boat building instructions so that he and his family could be saved.

- By faith, Abraham moved out of his settled life in Iraq and became the father of Israel.

- By faith, Sarah became a mommy well beyond her child-bearing years.

- By faith, Moses led God's people out of Egypt via the floor of the Red Sea and brought them to the edge of the Promised Land.

- By faith, Joshua blew not only the doors but the walls off of Jericho.

- By faith and a little red cord, a famous prostitute was saved from a destitute lifestyle and from Jericho's destruction, later becoming the great-great-grandmother of King David.

How much more do I need to say? It would take too long to recount the stories of the faith of Gideon, Barak, Samson, Jephthah, David, Samuel, and all the prophets. By faith these people overthrew kingdoms, ruled with justice, and received what God had promised them. They shut the mouths of lions, quenched the flames of fire, and escaped death by the edge of the sword. Their weakness was turned to strength. They became strong in battle and put whole armies to flight. Women received their loved ones back again from death. (Hebrews 11:32–35)

It is apparent that faith sometimes changes our circumstances. Men and women of faith throughout all generations can testify to positive turns in their circumstances because of their faith in God—perhaps a physical healing, perhaps a phenomenal solution to a dire financial need, perhaps a tough situation miraculously resolved, such as a strained relationship or a troubled marriage.

I have personally seen my share of positive turns of events through faith in God. My two-year-old nephew fell twenty feet head first onto concrete, only to be healed by God with no brain injuries whatsoever. Over the course of 30 years, one of my sisters and her husband have developed several significant faith-based ministries completely through trust in God's financial provision. I've seen my mother healed of a goiter by faith; one day, it just disappeared. I myself have received physical healing from God in my own body.

Even procuring my first teaching job was a miracle of God's provision. In my final year of teachers' college, even though I had applied to 100 job postings, I was having no success whatsoever. I believed I was following the Lord's leading through seven years of education, and I had faith that God would provide work, but my future looked bleak. Then, four days before the summer ended, I was hired by a board in a beautiful area near the city where I grew up. My application was one of 200, coincidentally the only one with a math and history teaching combination. Faith sometimes changes our circumstances, rearranging them for our good and for our comfort, ease, and pleasure.

But there is another observation regarding faith in this passage, an observation chillingly illustrated by a story from the life of my wife, Jeanette. Jeanette's dad was a farmer in northern Alberta. In 1957, he contracted a very serious form of leukemia. He became very sick very quickly. The family members and the entire church body came together in faith to pray for his recovery. Jeanette's mom had three children at the time and was pregnant with Jeanette. Two of their young children had died earlier in their story and there had already been a lot of grief and suffering—surely God would not allow this faithful woman to also lose her husband. And so they all prayed in faith . . . and they continued to pray . . . until October 23, 1957, when something remarkable happened: he died.

You see, life tells us, and the Scriptures testify, that faith sometimes does not change our circumstances. Sometimes it does, but sometimes it doesn't. Consider again our passage in Hebrews:

> *But others were tortured, refusing to turn from God in order to be set free. They placed their hope in a better life after the resurrection. Some were jeered at, and their backs were cut open with whips. Others were chained in prisons. Some died by stoning, some were sawed in half, and others were killed with the sword. Some went about wearing skins of sheep and goats, destitute and oppressed and mistreated. They were too good for this world, wandering over deserts and mountains, hiding in caves and holes in the ground. All these people earned a good reputation because of their faith, yet none of them received all that God had promised.*
> (Hebrews 11:35–39)

Many believers, past and present, have walked a life of pure and undefiled faith and yet have been called upon to pass through the fire of unchanged circumstances. Many have retained their faith in God but have not been delivered from their pain, their illnesses, or their heartaches.

In 1994, a good friend of ours died of cancer, leaving a husband and four children to mourn her passing. The story was tragic, involving an early misdiagnosis that spoiled her chances of survival. Both the husband and wife did everything right in the dying process. Their faith never wavered; together they clung to God, and she died. And God was pleased with them because faith pleases God—not wealth nor length of Christian service—just faith.

Our friend and her husband fought the good fight, they kept the faith. She finished her course and God was pleased with her. In God's loving sovereign will there are times when our circumstances don't improve from an earthly perspective.

But God calls us to different lengths of races. Some are called upon to do a marathon (Jeanette's grandma lived to 103), some a middle distance race, and some a short sprint.

Don't listen to anyone who tells you, "If you truly have faith, then your situation will improve." Faith is not that mystical, and there is no special formula. Have faith in God. Embrace him. Piggyback him and let the circumstances of your life fall as they may.

Are we confused when good Christian people are cut down in their prime? Of course. It is not how we humans think it should be done. John the Baptist was confused when he was being cut down in his prime. A young man around 30, cousin and boyhood friend of Jesus, he baptized the Messiah and proclaimed him to the world. He was at the peak of his ministry when he was thrown in jail and then eventually beheaded on the whim of an evil queen.

From our vantage point, we can understand John the Baptist's death now. He had to be removed in order for Jesus to start his kingdom. Otherwise, there would have been confusion and divided loyalties amongst the fickle followers of faith. We can see the big picture clearly now, but for John the Baptist, he simply had to have faith in God and experience the horror.

But our passage also provides us with an encouraging final observation regarding faith. The writer of Hebrews wanted us to know that faith always results in ultimate victory. Jesus leads the way for us in this one.

Therefore, since we are surrounded by such a huge crowd of witnesses to the life of faith, let us strip off every weight that slows us down, especially the sin that so easily trips us up. And let us run with endurance the race God has set before us. We do this by keeping our eyes on Jesus, the champion who initiates and perfects our faith. Because of the joy awaiting him, he endured the cross, disregarding its shame. Now he is seated in the place of honor beside God's throne. (Hebrews 12:1–2)

Jesus' work was accomplished, but it was a short ride. He was a mere 33 years of age when he was done. God's plan for him, the salvation of mankind, was finished. Jesus had faith in his Father and in his Father's plans. Yet, humanly, he didn't like it. *"My Father! If it is possible, let this cup of suffering be taken away from me. Yet I want your will to be done, not mine"* (Matthew 26:39).

For Jesus, there was ultimate victory after the suffering: sitting down at the right hand of the throne of God. And there is victory for us too. Faith always ends in ultimate victory. Our faith will take us to heaven, where we will one day be with our Savior. There will be no more tears and we will reign eternally as kings and priests in his kingdom. And even in this life, there is the ultimate victory of knowing that we are at peace with our Creator and that he is pleased with us.

Faith pleases God.

Faith sometimes changes our circumstances.

Faith sometimes does not change our circumstances.

Faith always results in ultimate victory.

For consider Him who has endured such hostility by sinners against Himself, so that you will not grow weary and lose heart. (Hebrews 12:3 NASB)

It's easy to lose heart in the midst of ongoing trials. Faith is not a part of our natural thought process, so we must continually consider Jesus. John the Baptist certainly lost heart in jail. In the midst of his suffering, John heard about the great miracles being performed by Jesus. He called his disciples to go question Jesus as to whether or not he was, in fact, the true Messiah. John must have thought, *If Jesus is for real, what am I doing in here? I should be out there with him.* John's faith was teetering. He must have asked himself many questions: *Did I get mixed up? Am I confused? Is this Jesus really the Son of God? Have I been believing a lie?*

Jesus' reply to his troubled cousin is both fascinating and challenging. He tells John's disciples to go back to the prophet and recount the many miracles being done by Jesus, but then he adds one final note. He says, "Hey fellas, I also want you to tell John this: *Blessed is he who keeps from stumbling over Me*" (Luke 7:23 NASB). What a strange comment. What is his point, you ask? Listen carefully. In essence, he is saying, "Blessed is he who does not get upset over the way I operate my business."

"Happy is the person who does not get disturbed over the way I run things." I believe that is the core principle of God's thoughts regarding faith.

Chapter 8

"Sooner or later, human pride will be humiliated."

"He is able to humble those who walk in pride."

~Daniel 4:37 NASB

Why are we so enamored with successful people? What is it about billionaires, professional sports stars, rock idols, movie celebrities, and political luminaries that makes us stop and ogle? Why do we want to glance at the tabloids as we go through the grocery line?

We have a natural affinity towards human greatness. We ourselves would like to be great. We are interested in the stories of people who have risen to the top of their game. Some of our megastars have a lot of talent while others have good connections. Some of them have brilliant ideas while others have a lot of luck. Some of them have countless hours of blood, sweat, and tears under their belts while others have steroids. No matter how a star rises, we cannot help but be fascinated with its persona. This is natural human thinking.

It is unfortunate that we expend so much energy tracking and adoring human greatness, because the game is so worldly.

Far too much human greatness is accompanied by human pride, and human pride has but one verdict: annihilation. Every arrogant sports star may have his spotlight and every supercilious diva her day, but sooner or later, human pride will be humiliated.

What does God think of us as we blatantly (and subtly) strut our stuff like silly little peacocks? Here's a hint: *"I hate pride and arrogance"* (Proverbs 8:13).

Human pride is so pitiable because it is based on the faulty illusion that greatness is both self-made and self-sustained. It is natural to believe that our noteworthy achievements have come about by our hard work. Notice the affirmation—it is natural. But this book is about the *supernatural*, about learning to think like God. It's about seeing and appreciating the other component that accompanies our hard work on the road to success.

One cannot talk about human pride without discussing the sovereignty of God. The sovereignty of God simply means that God is God and we are not. He is in complete control of the universe. To say he is huge would be an understatement of gargantuan proportions. We must avoid the mistake of putting him in a box that is limited to our understanding of him. He is not a white-bearded old man with some friendly advice for living. He is not our genie in a bottle, eagerly awaiting our demands. And he is not a weak but nice guy who feels sad and depressed about the direction of the world.

No, he is the sovereign Lord of the Universe and he is the sovereign Lord of every molecule in our bodies, keeping us from going insane and sustaining our hearts so they can beat 100,000 times every day. And the Lord of Creation will deal with our pride.

One day, every knee will bow to the sovereignty of God and to his exalted Son, Jesus Christ (Philippians 2:10–11). Do not be fooled; there will be no exceptions. It matters not what levels of health, wealth, or wisdom we attain; every human will submit to his authority. The trick to doing it right in life is to humble ourselves voluntarily to his rule before it's too late. Whether in life or in death, all human pride will be humiliated and we will kneel before God's sovereignty.

The book of Daniel tells a story of a man who learned this lesson . . . the hard way.

About 2,600 years ago, there lived a powerful king in the country of Babylonia (modern Iraq). His name was Nebuchadnezzar, and under his reign he established his kingdom as the dominant world power of the day. Initially, Nebuchadnezzar was not a believer in the one true God. He was a pagan man, and yet God, in his sovereignty, used him for a special plan.

At this point in history, God's chosen people, the children of Israel, were no longer following the Lord. In order to discipline them for their disobedience, God temporarily removed them from their homeland and subjected them to a period of captivity. To exact this punishment, God used Nebuchadnezzar as the conquering invader. *"Now I will give your countries to King Nebuchadnezzar of Babylon, who is my servant. I have put everything, even the wild animals, under his control"* (Jeremiah 27:6).

Nebuchadnezzar was not aware that he was part of a divine plan. He assumed that he was conquering, plundering, and expanding his kingdom by an act of his own will and personal determination. Was he ever way off! The book of Daniel records several interesting stories about this king and how he came to learn who runs the universe.

One day Nebuchadnezzar had a dream about a statue that had a gold head, silver chest and arms, bronze legs, and iron feet (Daniel 2). When the prophet Daniel interpreted the dream, it became apparent that God was showing the king important information about future world kingdoms. Instead of humbly honoring the Lord for choosing him to play a significant role in world history, Nebuchadnezzar became enthralled with himself and with the fact that, in the dream, God had referred to him as the golden head of the statue.

He then proceeded to build an entire statue in his likeness, made of gold and 90 feet high, commanding everyone in the kingdom to bow down to it or be torched in a fiery furnace. When three devout Hebrew lads refused to bow down to Nebuchadnezzar's statue, this great man turned into a great lunatic as his pride caused him to have a meltdown. *"Nebuchadnezzar was so furious . . . that his face became distorted with rage. He commanded that the furnace be heated seven times hotter than usual"* (Daniel 3:19). Of course, under God's sovereign control, the three Hebrews would not burn. Nebuchadnezzar was moved by the miracle (Daniel 3:29) but still had a long way to go before he was going to comprehend God's sovereignty.

You see, Nebuchadnezzar was a powerful man but he failed to understand why he was powerful. He had greatness and authority because God had put him in that position and granted him success. Unfortunately, he thought it was all his own doing.

Some time later, Nebuchadnezzar had another dream (Daniel 4) where a great tree, once strong and beautiful, was chopped down, stripped of its foliage, and cast into a dew-drenched field with the beasts of the earth. When Daniel interpreted this dream, it became apparent that God was warning Nebuchadnezzar of an impending personal humiliation.

Daniel informed Nebuchadnezzar that he, indeed, was the great tree, and his kingdom reached to the ends of the earth, visible to everyone, but because of his pride, he was going to be taken down and completely humiliated. Future activities were to involve the substantial consumption of grass and very little personal grooming. Solomon, in his wisdom, was right all along: *"Pride goes before destruction, and haughtiness before a fall"* (Proverbs 16:18).

The angel in the dream explained the purpose of the king's imminent disgrace.

For this has been decreed by the messengers; it is commanded by the holy ones, so that everyone may know that the Most High rules over the kingdoms of the world. He gives them to anyone he chooses – even to the lowliest of people. (Daniel 4:17)

Daniel pleaded with the king to improve his behavior in hopes that the Lord would change his mind about the punishment. *"Break from your wicked past,"* he cried (Daniel 4:27). But Nebuchadnezzar was destined for the lesson of his life—a lesson in brokenness.

The scriptural text says it best:

Twelve months later he was taking a walk on the flat roof of the royal palace in Babylon. As he looked out across the city, he said, "Look at this great city of Babylon! By my own mighty power, I have built this beautiful city as my royal residence to display my majestic splendor."

While these words were still in his mouth, a voice called down from heaven, "O King Nebuchadnezzar, this message is for you! You are no longer ruler of this kingdom. You will be driven from human society. You will live in the fields with the wild animals, and you will eat grass like a cow. Seven periods of time will pass while you live this way, until you learn that the Most High rules over the kingdoms of the world and gives them to anyone he chooses."

That same hour the judgment was fulfilled, and Nebuchadnezzar was driven from human society. He ate grass like a cow, and he was drenched with the dew of heaven. He lived this way until his hair was as long as eagles' feathers and his nails were like birds' claws. (Daniel 4:29–33)

Can you imagine the chatter in his royal court for those seven years? The stories, the cover-ups, the scandals? People asking "Where's the king?" "Oh, he's not feeling well lately; he's a bit under the weather" (literally). Imagine a great and powerful leader of our day going insane and crawling around on all fours, munching grass with bird-claw fingernails.

We need to grasp the danger of human pride. Know that God is in control and that his plan will be accomplished on earth—with or without our cooperation. God exalts whomever he chooses and he humbles whomever he wishes. Choose now to humble yourself before the Lord before it's too late. There is no guarantee that we will get another chance for restoration. Fortunately for Nebuchadnezzar, he did get another chance. Listen to what he learned.

After this time had passed, I, Nebuchadnezzar, looked up to heaven. My sanity returned, and I praised and worshiped the Most High and honored the one who lives forever. His rule is everlasting, and his kingdom is eternal. All the people of the earth are nothing compared to him.

He does as he pleases among the angels of heaven and among the people of the earth. No one can stop him or say to him, "What do you mean by doing these things?" When my sanity returned to me, so did my honor and glory and kingdom. My advisers and nobles sought me out, and I was restored as head of my kingdom, with even greater honor than before. Now I, Nebuchadnezzar, praise and glorify and honor the King of heaven. All his acts are just and true, and he is able to humble the proud. (Daniel 4:34–37)

What a great student! He learned his lesson and responded well. His pride was brought into submission. How might this God-like thinking work its way into our lives? What are the areas of pride in our lives that need to be stripped away like Nebuchadnezzar's foliage?

Are we bright? Are we rich? Are we talented? Are we successful in athletics, the arts, music, or business? God has given us these abilities for his glory, not ours. Rein in human pride. What God has given, he can so easily take away. However, just knowing these facts is not good enough. We need to act upon this knowledge and fall humbly before the Lord, being willing to obey his righteous commands. Humility and holiness are natural bedfellows.

The sad part of Nebuchadnezzar's happy ending is that his son, Belshazzar, witnessed the entire spectacular ordeal of his father's humiliation and conversion but did not act properly in response to this knowledge. Years later, when he himself was the supreme Babylonian ruler, Belshazzar threw a big party in which he arrogantly flaunted his position and authority, mocking the God of Israel. God crashed the party and wrote a message of doom on the wall for the king and his kingdom.

As Daniel interpreted the hand-writing, he scolded the king for his arrogance. He reminded him of his dad's experience and then said:

> *You are his successor, O Belshazzar, and you knew all this, yet you have not humbled yourself. For you have proudly defied the Lord of heaven . . . praising gods of silver, gold, bronze, iron, wood, and stone—gods that neither see nor hear nor know anything at all. But you have not honored the God who gives you the breath of life and controls your destiny!* (Daniel 5:22–23)

The message for Belshazzar was succinct: God has numbered the days of your reign and has brought them to an end. You have been weighed on the balances and have not measured up. Your kingdom has been divided and given to the Medes and Persians. That very night Belshazzar was killed (Daniel 5:25–28, 30). He knew better, but he didn't want to submit to divine authority. And then he paid the price for that poor choice.

We must take time to stop and think deeply about this subject. We need to examine our hearts and our minds and ask the Lord to cleanse them of human pride. We should think about God's sovereignty as much as he does. There is never any confusion in his mind about who is in control of the universe as well as who directs each of our steps (Proverbs 20:24).

And as the Lord goes about his business, we will not fully understand all that he is doing. At times we will be frustrated, and we will demand immediate justice for the flauntings of a proud person in our life. Do not be discouraged with the Lord's patience. Occasionally you will witness displays of arrogance that are allowed to linger. God gives us many chances to repent. He is slow to anger, not wanting any to perish. For now, we will continue to live amongst unrepentant pride, but only for a time. Isaiah reminds us that there is an impending day, the Day of the Lord, when all the injustices and unrighteousness will be corrected, when the proud will be laid low.

Human pride will be brought down, and human arrogance will be humbled. Only the Lord will be exalted on that day of judgment. For the Lord of Heaven's Armies has a day of reckoning. He will punish the proud and mighty and bring down everything that is exalted. (Isaiah 2:11–12)

Humble yourself before the Lord that he might exalt you at the right time in his plan. Humble yourself before the Lord while there is still time. We must understand what God thinks about human pride.

Chapter 9

"Sin is sneakier than you think, but it can be mastered."

"Sin is lying in wait for you, ready to pounce;
it's out to get you, you've got to master it."

~Genesis 4:7 MSG

We will always be dumber than our sin.

If we think we can win a head game against that rascal, we are sorely mistaken. In our natural state, sin is our master. We are its slave. We cannot not sin. And the more we sin, the dumber we get. We start panting more and more for the creation rather than the Creator. Regular and repeated sinful practices make our brains do dim-witted things. After a while we cannot tell what is right and wrong. What once seemed morally obvious to us in elementary school is now a mysterious ambiguity as a veteran sinning adult.

Without divine intervention, what a sorry state we find ourselves in! Not only are we powerless to resist sin's temptations, but sin ultimately leads to death—death to relationship, death to character, death to integrity, and inevitably, spiritual death, involving eternal separation from God.

When we begin to think like God, we come to understand that sin is the root of every human problem. Every educational, health care, and political crisis has its foundation in selfishness and disregard for the commands of a holy God. Every relational disaster we have ever created or weathered originates in sin. Social and economic problems are never caused by love, joy, peace, patience, kindness, goodness, faithfulness, gentleness, and self-control.

So, sin is clearly the enemy, and it resides in us from birth. Such a claim may offend some who struggle to see selfishness in the cooing eyes of a young baby. But once a child possesses the physical strength and verbal skill to express his or her opinion on a matter, that sinful nature latent within is not difficult to spot.

Somewhere in the mind of God, a plan was hatched that would have him take care of our sin problem, not we ourselves. Unlike religious schemes in human minds, we would not save ourselves. God would stoop down and save us from the mess we found ourselves in. God, through his Son, would deal with our sin problem.

The Bible clearly tells us how Christ's death was the perfect sacrifice for our sin, the atonement that satisfied a blameless God. The Father's holy and righteous wrath had to be appeased for us to have a hope of experiencing life after death. In our natural unforgiven state, God can only punish us. When the saving blood of Jesus is washed over our souls through repentance, God then sees us and treats us like his own children.

And something happens to our sin nature. The Apostle Paul describes it as a death and resurrection experience. Our old self is crucified with Christ so that it is potentially rendered powerless, no longer able to enslave us (Romans 6:6). So, then, why do so many of us who want to follow after Christ still seem to have a sin problem? Why does it appear that, in certain areas of our lives, sin still has its hands on the steering wheel? Why would the greatest of all apostles write *"I want to do what is good, but I don't. I don't want to do what is wrong, but I do it anyway"* (Romans 7:19)?

As usual, the problem is not with God and his promises but with our tendency to think humanly about matters that require a divine perspective. Once we have been saved and the initial period of spiritual elation passes, life settles into routines. These routines (work, marriage, child-rearing, church attendance) tend to eventually bring out the worst in us because of the incredible deception and trickiness of sin.

Consider the example of Cain in the earliest narratives of Scripture. What was going on when God warned him to be careful about sin getting ready to pounce on him? Was he living a life of immorality? Was he being disrespectful to his parents? On the surface, he probably looked like a pretty good guy. When it came time to offer sacrifices to God, he most likely worked hard at putting together his finest collection of fruits and vegetables. But God had no regard for his sacrifice.

Now, whether he was supposed to bring an animal sacrifice like Abel had done (*"without the shedding of blood there is no forgiveness"* Hebrews 9:22 NIV), or whether he was supposed to have a different attitude accompanying the offering, God's exhortation makes it clear that Cain knew he was doing something wrong. But the sin within Cain was deceptively having its way with this young man. One way or the other, Cain had decided to do his own thing rather than God's thing, and then he justified his behavior in his own mind regarding his choice and the unfairness of the situation.

Instead of repenting and doing God's will, Cain became angry with God and with his brother. Jealous rage led quickly to premeditated murder, and sin had won out. As God had warned, sin had become Cain's master; he was enslaved to its choices.

What mind games we play with sin! Like Cain, we rationalize, justify, and claim entitlement. We know behaviors are wrong, but perhaps not for us, not today, not in this particular situation. Even though Christ has disarmed sin's power for us, we continually volunteer our services to this old master. There is something tragic about this situation, and it is rooted in wrong thinking. The two tenets of poor human thinking in this area are: 1) that sin is not sneaky, and 2) that we can handle it ourselves.

As usual, there will be a God-thinking solution to this problem, but let us consider an illustration that may help us understand how sin operates when our thinking is wrong.

When I was a young teenager, my parents and I traveled 2,000 miles cross the country to attend a college graduation ceremony for my brother and oldest sister. Because we were far from home, the college allowed guests to stay in the dormitory and eat their meals in the cafeteria throughout the multi-day affair.

The food in the dining hall was not stellar, but we appreciated the free hospitality. However, my moment of reckoning came with the Saturday noon meal. It was an unusually warm April day for the Canadian prairies, and the cafeteria was serving one of its classics—breaded veal cutlets. Foolishly, I took two. I thought I was hungry and they looked somewhat appetizing.

As I began to consume them, I realized that something was not right with the whole dining experience. My stomach started to feel a little funny, but I had this engrained habit of finishing everything on my plate, so I pushed on and completed the task, amidst the increasingly thick and stuffy atmosphere of the non-air-conditioned food services building.

By the time I swallowed the last morsels of the cutlets, I no longer thought something was wrong—I *knew* something was wrong. My stomach was now churning like an egg beater. The warm, smelly air around me, coupled with the heat erupting within me, felt overwhelming.

At that moment, I knew what had to be done. What needed to be determined quickly was, of course, location—the key point to every good vomit story. Where was I going to make my deposit? I quickly sized up the situation and determined my options. The dining hall floor did not seem like a good choice, as I was afraid it might set off a chain reaction. I wasn't aware of the location of a bathroom within the building so I headed outside.

Instead of just doing the deed in the bushes outside the door, my mind took me to a washroom in the dormitory where I was staying. It was a mere fifty-meter dash across the lawn to the dorm and I would be home free. In retrospect, the bushes just outside the door would have been a much wiser choice, but when you get a plan in your head in these crisis situations, you tend to stick with it. I moved hastily towards the dorm. When you are about to throw up, you don't usually run; you walk incredibly briskly, carefully concentrating on holding it back.

These situations markedly display the epic battle between self-control and nature. Will I be able to control myself until I reach the great white throne, or will the powerful natural processes of my body override my timing? Well, in this case, as experienced by many others before me, both small and great, nature won the battle!

I made it up the stairs into the lobby. I turned right, going towards the hallway, then left down the hallway. The bathroom was just seconds away when, all of a sudden, I did a five-foot projectile right onto the carpet ahead of me, just outside the bathroom door.

What humiliation! What relief! You know that feeling when you are about to throw up—the sensation that you are about to die. Well, now I felt better, but I was starting to wish I had died, as people came to see what the commotion was all about. For the rest of the weekend, I was known as Phil Olney's little brother who puked all over the dorm hallway.

I should have known better. I fooled myself, thinking I could make it, thinking I could win the battle. It's funny how we try to resist throwing up. We always want to hold off as long as we can. And yet nature always wins. If our body tells us it is time to throw up, we will most likely throw up. There's not a lot we can do about it.

Now to the spiritual point of my saga. I think we can liken the natural urge to vomit to our natural urge to sin. Our attempt to hold back the . . . material, is like our attempt to not sin. In our own strength, we are not going to win the battle. Again, the Apostle Paul speaks to this issue:

> *I don't really understand myself, for I want to do what is right, but I don't do it. Instead, I do what I hate . . . And I know that nothing good lives in me, that is, in my sinful nature. I want to do what is right, but I can't . . . Oh, what a miserable person I am! Who will free me from this life that is dominated by sin and death?* (Romans 7:15, 18, 24)

Committing your life to following Jesus as your Savior and Lord does not mean that he forgives you of your sin so that you can go off and try to live *your* Christian life to the best of *your* ability. Living a successful Christian life has very little to do with *your* ability at all.

Many Christian believers walk in defeat instead of victory because they fail to understand the true nature of salvation. They think salvation makes them a better person who is now able to resist sin more effectively. This is not true. Becoming a Christian does not make you a better person at all. A Christian is capable of committing any of the same sins as a non-Christian.

The real difference is that a Christian is capable of not sinning. But understand this—God's thoughts on human holiness are centered on his precious Son, not on human endeavor. The best explanation of this principle is given by the Apostle Paul in his letter to the Galatian church:

> *I have been crucified with Christ; and it is no longer I who live, but Christ lives in me; and the life which I now live in the flesh I live by faith in the Son of God, who loved me and gave Himself up for me.* (Galatians 2:20 NASB)

Another translation says it this way:

*Christ lives in me. The life you see me living is not "mine,"
but it is lived by faith in the Son of God, who loved me and
gave himself for me.* (MSG)

A non-Christian is compelled to sin in the face of overwhelming temptation; there is no power to resist when the
attraction grips the heart. A Christian, on the other hand,
possesses the possibility of resisting sin, but only through faith
in Christ, letting him live his life through us.

In his *Handbook to Happiness*, Dr. Charles Solomon refers
to this concept as "the exchanged life."[2] Human thinking
would have a believer maintain the approach of "trying to live
the Christian life," with a focus on human effort. Instead, we
need to allow Christ to live his life through us by faith. This is
the truth that leads to victory over sin's domination, enabling
us to live a holy life before God and man.

But what does this mean? What needs to be done practically
for it to happen?

We resist some sins in our lives out of habit or fear of
getting caught. Other sins are easily discarded because they do
not seem to resonate with any sort of attraction within our
bevy of appetites. But there is a level of sin in each of our
lives that is so potent, so compelling, that we cannot overcome
it by our own strength. It is too delicious; it offers too many
temporary but powerful rewards. Even though, on paper, we
hate the sin, we love the rush it gives us. We must, or we
wouldn't keep going back to the trough. Everyone seems to
have at least one area of struggle in their life that just won't go
away.

This level of sin cannot be overcome by an act of the
human will. Even though we marshal all our own troops into
one seemingly strong assembly, we will lose the battle over
and over, just like I lost the battle to those cutlets so many
years ago. Instead of fighting, this deep level of sinful

---

[2] Dr. Charles Solomon, *Handbook to Happiness* (Carol Stream, IL: Tyndale House
Publishers, 1999), 120.

struggle is overcome by surrender—surrender to the life of Christ within us as children of God.

When we are faced with that familiar temptation to sin, we need to pray: "By faith, Lord Jesus, I am asking you to live your life through me right now; at this moment, don't let me live my life or I will fall, I will sin."

Living by faith means we, as new creations, can call on our Savior to deliver us from any sin any moment of the day. By faith, we believe that, through the Holy Spirit, the indwelling Christ can live his life through us, thus emasculating sin's hold on us. When we allow Christ to live his life though us, we will not sin because *he* cannot sin.

As believers, we need to stop fooling ourselves into thinking we can handle sin on our own. We can't. It's far too sneaky. And like Cain, it is always ready to pounce on us. Stop trying to resist it in your own strength. Cry out in faith to our God, who wants to use you as a vessel for his wonderful Son, and you will find yourself walking in victory and joy and peace.

A word of caution, though: just as we learned to walk as a baby over a period of time, learning to walk by faith is also a process that takes time. We will stumble and fall, but the more we practice faith, the more naturally it will emerge in our response to temptation and the more commonly our actions will reflect the character God has supernaturally called us to display.

Chapter 10

"Integrity is everything."

*"I know, my God, that you examine our hearts
and rejoice when you find integrity there."*

~1 Chronicles 29:17

I have had problems with a weak left shoulder joint since 1986. In the winter of that year, I dislocated it for the first time in a hockey game. It was quite uneventful and unheroic. No one hit me; I just tripped over my own skates and fell forward. When I put my arms out in front of me to catch myself, my left shoulder popped out of joint. Fortunately, we had a chiropractor on our team and he relocated it back into place on the bench.

Following that incident, I went through three years of various therapies and different forms of conditioning, but to no avail. My shoulder kept popping out regularly—a couple more times in hockey, once playing basketball, once even vacuuming the car.

By 1989, I had had enough of the failed strengthening program, so I secured a good shoulder surgeon who was able to repair the torn capsule that was failing to keep the joint secure. The surgery went very well and, after about three months of recovery and physiotherapy, I was back to playing hockey and basketball again. I had no problems for the next ten years.

Then, in 1999, my fortunes were reversed. The scene was a church hockey league play-off game. We were down a goal, and I was making a hard left turn to break to the net when an opponent wrapped his arm over my left arm and pulled me down to the ice. The force of the check yanked my shoulder out of joint, re-tearing the capsule again. Well, there I was—back to square one.

For the next seven years, until my second surgery in 2006, I continued to play sports but did so carefully, always protecting my shoulder. In hockey, I wore a brace; in basketball, I rebounded and played defense with only one arm. I was always conscious of my left shoulder's weakness and instability, even when I used it to merely push open a door.

In the midst of that seven-year period, my shoulder even dislocated a few times in my sleep. It was quite traumatic to wake up in the middle of the night in excruciating pain with the joint out of place. Eventually, the drama ended with a successful second repair job in the spring of 2006. Since then, it has stayed in place and I am cautiously optimistic about it remaining that way.

This type of athletic injury is odd. When the bone is out of the socket, the pain is piercing. When it is put back in place, the suffering is instantly gone (except for a dull ache for a few days). During those pre-surgery years, my shoulder always looked fine on the outside—no one could see a problem by just looking at me. But on the inside, my shoulder was weak and unstable, unable to handle the harsher demands of life. Until the torn capsule was repaired, my shoulder could not withstand any real stress at all. Outward appearances can be deceptive.

This description of my damaged shoulder parallels the condition of some people's lives. On the surface, they appear okay, but inside, there is a problem—a weakness and instability with an accompanying lack of rich, spiritual character.

As a human, my natural tendency is to think about whether or not I look okay on the outside; but as a Christian, I should be more concerned about the inside, my true character. That's what God is thinking about. I know that what matters ultimately is who I am at the very core of my being. The word we often use to describe this inner character, this deep necessary purity, is integrity.

In a nutshell, you can gauge your integrity by a simple two-part test. First, consider the nature of your thought life: what are the predominate topics that fill your mind? Second, what do you do when no one is looking? Who are you when you know that no one can see you, when you think that no one will find out what you are doing? How do you behave? What are the things you like to do if you believe you can do them with impunity?

Integrity is a significant dynamic in God's thoughts on human behavior. We would do well to think sincerely about this topic. But what exactly does integrity mean? My dictionary defines integrity as "moral excellence, honesty, wholeness, and soundness." [3]

It is quite obvious that a person with integrity demonstrates moral excellence. For instance, a person with integrity displays the highest regard for the character and behavioral traits outlined by God in his Word. Such a person controls their tongue so that it does not hurt others unnecessarily. A person with integrity is humble and can be trusted to do what she promised.

A person with integrity respects people's property, whether it belongs to a neighbor or a mean, miserly boss. When tax time rolls around, a person of integrity claims all of his income for the year, even from the hidden sources. And, certainly, a person of integrity respects the sexual purity of others in relationships both before and during marriage. In

---

[3] *The Oxford Dictionary of Current English* (Oxford: Oxford University Press, 1992), 460.

other words, a person with integrity demonstrates moral excellence.

One of the Psalm writers expresses it this way,

I will lead a life of integrity in my own home. I will refuse to look at anything vile and vulgar. I hate all who deal crookedly; I will have nothing to do with them. I will reject perverse ideas and stay away from every evil. I will not tolerate people who slander their neighbors. I will not endure conceit and pride. (Psalm 101:2-5)

We need others to continually challenge us about our private activities. What are we looking at in the seclusion of our own homes? Is there anything vile or vulgar in our story? What kind of reputation have we established in our families, neighborhoods, churches, and workplaces? People of integrity display an unswerving and transparent life of moral excellence.

Besides moral excellence, people with integrity are also honest in all their dealings. Integrity means returning that extra ten-dollar bill or even a quarter that the cashier mistakenly gave you as change from your purchase. People of integrity speak the truth, regardless of the occasion or the audience. They strive to tell the same story with their mouth that their life is living in private. Their public speech and their personal life mirror each other.

Take time to think about this. Do we find ourselves in a position where we are regularly covering up things we have done? Are there skeletons in our closets that we are presently lying about to others in order to mask the true nature of our character? We must not be mistaken; we may fool some people for a long or a short while, but rest assured, the truth will find us out eventually and our crooked path of deception will bring us to some form of ruin. Solomon warns us, *"People with integrity walk safely, but those who follow crooked paths will slip and fall"* (Proverbs 10:9).

In the mind of God, honesty is a very crucial part of Christian integrity. From a practical standpoint, the cool thing about telling the truth is that you never have to remember what you said . . . because it was the truth and there is nothing to cover-up.

So, integrity involves moral excellence and honesty, but it also involves wholeness and soundness. These two ideas are very closely related.

Certainly, the mathematical term "integer" comes from the same root word as integrity, and we all know (or at least we did when we were in grade seven) that integers deal with positive and negative "whole" numbers as opposed to fractions and messy decimals. A person with integrity has a sense of wholeness or completeness. The inside is as solid as the outside. A person with integrity may be described as one with sound character.

It is no surprise that we associate wholeness with soundness and sound character. What is the difference in sound between hitting something whole and solid as opposed to hitting something hollow? Have you ever tapped on drywall or paneling in an attempt to find a solid stud behind the wall surface in order to hang up a heavy picture? There is a distinct difference in the sound produced.

And how about termites? I've heard that termites can ravish the wood in a house so that it still looks okay on the outside but internally is on the verge of collapse. The floor beams look strong, but when you tap them, you hear the emptiness, the hollowness of the termites' work. If someone were to tap on us right now, what sound would we make? If someone were to tap on the shell or exterior of the spiritual life that we regularly display, what would they hear? Would it make a hollow noise, or would there be the sound of wholeness, completeness, and integrity through and through?

You see, our lives can be a lot like my shoulder joint in its questionable period. We look fine on the outside but we lack internal integrity. In its unrepaired state, my shoulder could handle the normal routines of life but it could not deal with any kind of duress. During those bad periods, if I played sports with any kind of aggression, it was coming out of joint. If I lifted something awkward or heavy over my head, it could easily pop out. If someone even bumped my arm while it was extended in a vulnerable position, I was in for another dislocation.

As a Christian, if we are simply okay on the outside, we may be able to handle the normal demands of life. But what happens when we have to face real trials and heartbreaking hardships beyond our comprehension? When there is a deficiency in integrity, we lack the wholeness and soundness to be able to cope. We will collapse. We will dislocate.

There are a certain amount of "living in a fallen world" challenges that the average person can deal with in their own human strength, but when tremendous disappointments and painful sorrows attack us mercilessly, our true character will undergo a test and it will be manifest for what it actually is. If our lives were to begin to unravel today, would our internal character pass the test?

As opposed to the one who collapses in ruin under duress, the Christian who lives a life of steady moral excellence, honesty, and sound character will, on the other hand, be able to stand in God's strength amidst a world that is falling apart. What a blessing to have a consistent lifestyle and reputation of integrity, especially during the hard times.

Psalm 119:1–3 says, *"Joyful are people of integrity, who follow the instructions of the Lord. Joyful are those who obey his laws and search for him with all their hearts. They do not compromise with evil, and they walk only in his paths."* In fact, when we walk in integrity, even our children are promised a divine blessing. Proverbs 20:7 reads: *"The godly walk with integrity; blessed are their children who follow them."*

Now, as we ponder this important subject, we need to remember that integrity and sound character do not come to us solely by our own effort as we strive to be good. As we discussed in the previous chapter, it comes through an enduring and challenging walk of faith in Jesus Christ. The effort we make is largely confession, dying to self, and surrendering, consistently letting him live his life through us in every situation of the day. We referred to this as the "exchanged life" and have already elaborated on its principles as presented in Galatians 2:20.

And so, we need to examine our hearts. Where there has been deceit and hollowness, we need to confess our sins to the Lord—and to one another if necessary and appropriate. If we have been living a dual life of deception, today we need to begin walking in integrity

We are in desperate need of Jesus. He is the Savior of all mankind. He is our deliverer. That is why he came and that is why he died and rose again: to make us holy and to make us whole, through and through. Jesus wants to save each of us from a life of sinful filthiness as well as a life of pretend holiness. He wants us to be pure, whole, and rich in character, right down to the core.

Let us consider our present condition and repent before God. Let us respond quickly and appropriately before a harsh trial arrives in our lives, one that exposes the hollowness and lack of integrity, causing our world to collapse like a colossal skyscraper constructed on a flimsy foundation of toothpicks. We need to move forward from wherever we find ourselves. We need to let Jesus be the surgeon and let him repair the weaknesses within so that we may be truly holy and our character may be strong.

Because we have a God who knows all, integrity is everything!

Chapter 11

"It's dangerous in the dark."

*"Those who walk in darkness cannot see
where they are going."*

~John 12:35

There is a bold and blatant contrast between God's thoughts and man's thoughts regarding darkness and light. *"God is light, and in Him there is no darkness at all"* (1 John 1:5 NASB). *"But men loved darkness instead of light because their deeds were evil"* (John 3:19 NIV).

God is pure light. Naturally, we try to stay out of the light. In our fallen state, we veer away from his brightness because it exposes our weaknesses, our shortcomings. We are embarrassed for light to be shone upon some of our deeds because they are . . . well, embarrassing.

But there is often a sense of cockiness in our perception of our situation. Frequently, we have an exaggerated sense of our own security and safety as we ignore God's thinking regarding darkness. What we really need to understand is that, if we play around in the dark, we are not nearly as safe as we think we are.

I learned a little something about the dangers of darkness when I was in my early forties. I was the principal of a residential high school that had regular weekend activities for the students. One Friday night, the activity of choice was Mission Impossible, a game of chasing and catching your opponents in the dark. I can't remember the specific rules of the game but I remember a lot about that night. Clearly, I had an exaggerated perception of my own abilities to not only run fast, but to operate successfully in the dark.

Here are the lessons I learned.

First of all, in the dark, you make a lot of poor decisions. As I was hiding in the bushes and ravines, I would try to calculate the best angle for intercepting approaching students. Most of the time I messed up or failed to catch anybody. As I encountered groups of students, I was forced to decide which one to chase as they scattered in all directions. Inevitably, I would choose the track star, who would leave me in the dust.

I also realized that, in the dark, you don't always know who you are dealing with. Throughout much of the game, I didn't know who I was chasing. On two occasions, I tackled someone who was just out for a night-time jog and wasn't part of the game at all. And twice I jumped another teacher who was on my team. It was painfully evident that I did not know who I was dealing with.

On that fateful night I was also reminded of the fact that, in the dark, you cannot see what is ahead of you. At one point in the game, I was pursuing a student wearing a long trench coat; it was flying gracefully behind him. As I gained ground on him, I excitedly reached out to grab the coat in victory when suddenly I was greeted by a six-foot evergreen. Wham! Right in the face. I wiped out and tumbled to the ground. Fortunately, I wasn't hurt, and even better, nobody saw it happen, so I could pop right up without having to look around and feel stupid.

Now, as I said, I wasn't hurt—but my evening wasn't over yet. And it wasn't long before I learned that, in the dark, you *can* get hurt. A few minutes later, I was chasing a couple of girls. Again, as I reached out to grab the slower of the two, I was intercepted by a guy wire attached to another tree. As my shin connected with the wire, I went airborne and did a face plant on the ground. Needless to say, when we returned to school on Monday morning, the students had a joyful time teasing me about my all-too-visible battle scars.

The lessons I learned about operating in the dark that fateful Friday night playing Mission Impossible have a very natural transference to the concept of spiritual darkness. God has clearly revealed to us his thoughts on spiritual darkness and light. The point of his salvation plan is to call us *"out of darkness into his wonderful light"* (1 Peter 2:9), or as the Apostle Paul says, *"he has rescued us from the kingdom of darkness and transferred us into the Kingdom of his dear Son"* (Colossians 1:13). Once the heavenly transaction is complete, living in the light looks like this:

> *Let there be no sexual immorality, impurity, or greed among you. Such sins have no place among God's people. Obscene stories, foolish talk, and coarse jokes—these are not for you. Instead, let there be thankfulness to God. You can be sure that no immoral, impure, or greedy person will inherit the Kingdom of Christ and of God. For a greedy person is an idolater, worshiping the things of this world. Don't be fooled by those who try to excuse these sins, for the anger of God will fall on all who disobey him. Don't participate in the things these people do. For once you were full of darkness, but now you have light from the Lord. So live as people of light! For this light within you produces only what is good and right and true. Carefully determine what pleases the Lord. Take no part in the worthless deeds of evil and darkness; instead, expose them. It is shameful even to talk about the things that ungodly people do in secret. But their evil intentions will be exposed when the light shines on them, for the light makes everything visible. This is why it is said, "Awake, O sleeper, rise up from the dead, and Christ will give you light."* (Ephesians 5:3–14)

When we shun the light of the gospel, refusing the gift of salvation in Jesus Christ, we are walking in spiritual darkness and we are headed for destruction. When we, as believers, dabble in the deeds of darkness from our past, we are also in a lot more danger than we may realize.

When we walk in spiritual darkness, we make very poor decisions. Our brain gets messed up by sin—right looks wrong and wrong looks right. We can't think straight. We are more easily fooled by the devil. Intentional exposure to harmful substances (from chemicals to porn) creates addictions and twisted thought patterns that lead to even poorer decision-making.

Such habit-forming activities also impede the normal operation of our conscience. Our God-given warning mechanism becomes seared to a point where it no longer triggers proper remorse and regret. Darkness causes us to make compounding poor decisions. That is why Jesus said, *"I am the light of the world. If you follow me, you won't be stumbling through the darkness, because you will have the light that leads to life"* (John 8:12).

I also learned that, when we are in the dark, we do not always know who we are dealing with. The same is true for spiritual darkness. When we are walking in spiritual darkness, apart from the guiding hand of God and the light of his Word, we may think we are out there on our own, but we're not. We may see ourselves as our own man, our own woman, forging the path of our own choosing by our own will. But the truth of the matter is that we may not be the one who is actually steering the course of our life at all.

Apart from God, we are subject to the influence and control of the devil and his demons. The Apostle Paul warns us,

> *Satan, who is the god of this world, has blinded the minds of those who don't believe. They are unable to see the glorious light of the Good News. They don't understand this message about the glory of Christ, who is the exact likeness of God.* (2 Corinthians 4:4)

In the dark, we do not know who we are dealing with, and there are a lot of spiritual forces at work around us. When we are outside the light of Christ, there is no protection from the power and sway of dark demonic forces on our lives.

We must understand, if we are walking in paths of spiritual darkness, we are not dealing with God, we are dealing with the other guy. And this is not a simple Star Wars adventure of going over to the dark side for a while; this is the battle for our eternal souls. The Apostle Paul was told by God that his calling in life was to go to the Gentiles *"to open their eyes, so they may turn from darkness to light and from the power of Satan to God"* (Acts 26:18).

Earlier in this chapter, I also mentioned that, in the dark, we have trouble seeing what is ahead of us. Those who walk in spiritual darkness apart from Christ cannot see impending consequences. When we dwell in spiritual darkness, it is difficult to see the ramifications of sin.

What might be obvious to a heart that is tender towards God is a mystery to the unconverted. There is no way the unregenerate heart can perceive what sin is going to do to them, for they are in the dark. Sexual inappropriateness is just for fun, alcohol and drugs are just toys, and dabbling in the occult is just a joke. The byproducts of sin—STDs, brain damage, broken relationships, destroyed families, and demonic oppression and possession—are simply neither anticipated nor considered by people walking in darkness. They can't see it coming.

As well, those dwelling in spiritual darkness are totally oblivious to the imminent return of Jesus Christ and the judgment that will follow this great cataclysmic event. As Paul says to the Thessalonian church, the great Day of the Lord will overtake those in darkness like a thief in the night (1 Thessalonians 5). Darkness impairs forward vision, both physically and spiritually.

But darkness also guarantees pain. Those operating in the dark will eventually get hurt. Living in spiritual darkness without Christ will inevitably result in a great deal of suffering that words cannot begin to describe. Besides the sorrowful consequences of sin in this world, those outside of the light of Christ will experience eternal hurt.

Talking about hell is not a popular subject these days, even within the church. Our brains and hearts have a hard time grasping what it means to suffer forever, so we choose not to think about it. But that detracts from the truth—hell is real, and it is prepared for those who walk in darkness.

In eternity, the enemies of God will get what they clamored for throughout their earthly existence: separation from him. Those who walk in darkness now are destined for eternal darkness in hell. Sadly, I have heard some non-Christians cavalierly jest about hell and about their belief that it will not be such a bad place; after all, they will have all their buddies there. They envision their eternity as some sort of splendid celebration for all those free thinkers who courageously lived their own lives apart from religious restrictions and hang-ups and boldly flipped God the bird on their deathbed.

Bad idea.

The Scriptures give no picture of hell as some sort of grand central party station for a bunch of good-ole boys. Rather, images of hell are unspeakably horrific: they include separation from God (2 Thessalonians 1:9 and Matthew 7:23); unquenchable fires (Mark 9:43); everlasting worms (Isaiah 66:24); gloomy pits of the blackest darkness (2 Peter 2:4, 17); eternal destruction (2 Thessalonians 1:9); anguish that produces weeping and gnashing of teeth (Matthew 8:12); and a place of torment (Luke 16:28), wrath, and fury (Romans 2:8), with no relief day or night (Revelation 14:11). Jesus clearly explained that going to hell is far worse than having your body parts sliced off or your eye gouged out in this life (Matthew 5:29–30). The last book of the Bible refers to it as the second death (Revelation 21:8).

Those who walk in spiritual darkness are in for eternal hurt. There are no two ways about it. We cannot afford to fool ourselves. It's dangerous in the dark.

My parents used to tell me—and I told my own children when they were teens—"Nothing much good happens after midnight." We as parents like to see our children at home and in bed by midnight because we know of the dangers after dark. So much crime and so many poor personal choices are made in the middle of the night by weary bodies and deceived brains.

Human thinking is still drawn to the dark. We are enamored with its mysteries and enticed by its secrecy. Or, again, as the Apostle John says, "*All who do evil hate the light and refuse to go near it for fear their sins will be exposed*" (John 3:20).

God, in his holiness, is pure brightness, and his Word is a lamp to guide our feet and a light for our path (Psalm 119:105). When we begin to think like God about the meaning and significance of spiritual light and darkness and their temporal as well as eternal consequences, it will be easier for us to become one of "*those who do what is right (who) come to the light so others can see that they are doing what God wants*" (John 3:21).

Chapter 12

"Stop flying below the radar."

"But everyone who denies me here on earth,
I will also deny before my Father in heaven."

~Matthew 10:33

When it comes to the importance of living your Christian life in public, Jesus does not beat around the bush. Confessing Christ openly is an integral part of our salvation (Matthew 10:32). If we claim to be followers of Christ but implicitly or subtly deny him before others, Christ will not vouch for us before God. If that doesn't scare you a little, maybe you need to read it again.

Jesus could not have said it more plainly:

I tell you the truth, everyone who acknowledges me publicly here on earth, the Son of Man will also acknowledge in the presence of God's angels. But anyone who denies me here on earth will be denied before God's angels. (Luke 12:8–9)

The message is clear and simple. Human thinking wants to embrace salvation as some sort of private gift that is kept a secret between the Savior and the saved. God-like thinking about salvation involves a more demonstrative approach to Christian expression. If you are a follower of Christ but no one knows it, his exhortation to you today is this: stop flying below the radar. In the Master's own words, *"Let your good deeds shine out for all to see, so that everyone will praise your heavenly Father"* (Matthew 5:16). Christian practice is not a stealth mission. There are no points for keeping it under wraps. Though it sounds cliché, this familiar question still holds great poignancy: If you were put on trial for being a Christian, would there be enough evidence to convict you?

Let us consider what it might mean to live our faith out loud as opposed to flying below the radar.

We need to think recurrently about how Christ can make us into better people. We need to keep our hearts soft towards God while at the same time thinking about what it means to become a potent person of impact. We can't use shyness or humility as an excuse for our inactivity and lethargy. We must cry out to God to give us confidence, a unique boldness that sees this world—though usurped by Satan temporarily—as actually belonging to our God. Let us pray for a fiery passion in our hearts to be far above average and the ordinary.

Many believers fail to see how they have the potential to be great people of impact. You see, it is really people that impact people. That's what should go on in homes, at church, at work—Christian people impacting their family, their neighbors, their peers. Every bit of learning should be seen as sacred and should be considered part of our preparation for serving in God's kingdom.

This world needs strong, confident, whole Christians who are trained by the Scriptures and energized by the power of the Holy Spirit to shake up this planet. When I was taking my master's degree in Education, I was reminded once again of the poverty of humanism. During one course in particular, Ethics and Social Responsibility, I had to read a fair bit of atheistic philosophy on the subject of ethics and morality. And frankly, I must say that it was quite pitiful to read brilliant scholars saying inane things as they tried desperately to fabricate some pretend meaning of life in their pathetic little world without God.

I am reminded time and time again of the bankruptcy of this world's system. As John says in his first epistle—the lust of the flesh, the lust of the eyes, and the boastful pride of life are all eventually passing away (1 John 2:15–17). This world has nothing new to offer: intoxicants, depression and despair, glittery distractions, and billions of pornographic sites.

As the prince of the power of the air (Ephesians 2:2), Satan makes this world look intelligent, attractive, and sophisticated, but it is, indeed, bankrupt. And it is our job as Christians to bring new money to the table and establish a new system. The new money is the gospel of Jesus Christ and the new system is the kingdom of God. I know that Jesus is the one who builds his kingdom, but we need some confident Peters and Pauls to set their faces aggressively into the headwind and do battle with the forces of spiritual darkness.

One of the best ways we can be a positive force in the building of God's kingdom is for us to have something decent and attractive to offer at the table for whatever it is that we are doing. The gospel should look attractive because of our lives. Jesus is beautiful. If people cannot see the beauty of Jesus in our lives, we are doing something wrong. We're hiding him.

I am a firm believer that Christians should be the best and brightest . . . at everything. Christians should be the nicest people in the group. Christian folk in the business world should have the most novel thoughts. Christians should have the most creative ideas for solutions to world problems.

Christians should be the best professionals, the best teachers in the school, the best doctors in the clinic, and the best optometrists in the office. Christians should be building the best families with the best reputations in the neighborhood. Christians should be the best and brightest public servants, the best communicators, and the best humorists. We should be the best actors and actresses and we should be coming up with the best and most creative music. We have a personal pipeline to the Creator of the Universe and the Maker of our souls. We, of all people, should be the most creative, the most innovative.

And yet, somehow, we have got this perverted, stolid idea that Christianity is all about conservativism. The only reason the word "liberal" sounds bad to an evangelical ear is because we have left it to the pagans to come up with the new ideas in life, many of which are not very good. And so we cling to old and outdated ideas that are now ineffective; they are all we have because we haven't created something new and fresh ourselves. Christians have not typically adapted well to change and become transformational leaders. We need to make sure that we do not prepare ourselves to be beautifully equipped for a world that does not exist.

I am not talking about tampering with the gospel or liberalizing the saving message of Christ, but certainly some of us should be able to figure out how to adorn the gospel in our lives in such a new and fresh way that people will fight to get a good look at us?

Attack this world with confidence, with power, and with faith. When Jesus sent his apostles out on a little preaching tour, as recorded in Matthew 10, he exhorted them to be shrewd as serpents and innocent as doves (v. 16). We are called to be holy, but not stupid and lazy. Be smart! Use all the molecules! Be a lifelong learner who is continually examining what you know and what you might know if you tried something new.

Granted, living in a fallen world is hard. It's disappointing at times, and discouragement can creep over us if we are not careful. But that is where faith comes in. We need to reread Hebrews 11 and 12 regularly to refresh our understanding of faith. We know that, without faith, it is impossible to please God. We also know faith sometimes changes our circumstances (David kills Goliath, the walls of Jericho fall down, the cancer goes into remission). But if we were to read those chapters carefully, we would also be reminded that faith sometimes does not change our circumstances (sometimes the imprisoned believer is tortured and killed and not delivered, sometimes jobs are lost and the money runs out, and sometimes the cancer kills, even though a million prayers were offered up in faith).

You see, faith is not a genie's lamp that, when rubbed, automatically gives us what we want. It is possible to live a full and active life of faith in God in the midst of things not working out very well for you. Surely you must know of believers who have chosen to be courageous in their response to tragedy. Instead of retreating into self-pity and a reclusion of sorrow, they rebound with a stupendous and aggressive act of faith.

Now that's being the best you can be. That's an attractive walk of faith. That is faith flowering into ultimate victory. Hey, that's what faith does—it wins!—not always in this world, but certainly in eternity. Faith gives you the confidence to go on and continue to make a powerful difference with your new and creative solutions to problems. The faith passage in Hebrews ends with these words:

> . . . *fixing our eyes on Jesus, the author and perfecter of faith, who for the joy set before him, endured the cross, despising the shame, and has sat down at the right hand of the throne of God. For consider him who has endured such hostility by sinners against himself, so that you may not grow weary and lose heart.* (Hebrews 12:2–3 NASB)

Think of the confidence with which Jesus tackled his mission, his calling, even though he knew it was going to involve unbelievable suffering, bearing the sin of the whole world on his shoulders. Now, you might say, "Well that was Jesus; he's the Son of God." But Jesus also told his followers that when he went back to heaven they would be equipped to do greater works than those done by him. When our faith in God causes us to be bold, to be creative, to not lose heart and give up, we are adorning the gospel, making it look attractive to the world.

I'm tired of weak, wimpy Christians flying below the radar, making no impact on their world as they act ashamed of their Savior, living life with no gusto whatsoever. We need to rid ourselves of the entanglements that are disqualifying us from being a player, those habits that are making us weak and embarrassed.

Why can't we tackle some issue around us with creativity? Is the language in our homes offensive? Create some way to fix it. Make a fun contest. Raise awareness of the seriousness of the issue through some creative format. Think about it. We could ask God to help us come up with a novel idea.

Think about our places of work; does Christ and his kingdom take a beating every lunch or break time? Are we apologetic for belonging to him or are we going to figure out a creative way to be bold in his defense without being arrogant jerks ourselves or coming across looking like crazy cult people?

Regardless of the toughness of our circumstances, faith can lead us to a life of victory. Let me give you a little illustration from the life of my youngest daughter, Heather. In her grade 11 year, I was inspired by her faith amidst a personal trial near the end of basketball season. It is a common tale in high school athletics—dad is the coach, daughter is the point guard. The season was going well but drawing to a close. We had finished first in the league that year with a record of 10–2 and we were in the semi-finals of the city play-offs when Heather went down near the end of the third quarter with a broken leg. Heather was the top scorer on the team and in the league, our top assist getter, and had a 9.8 steals-per-game average. Needless to say, she was an impact player on our team. Well, we hung on to win the semi-final game but ended up losing the city finals, the district championship, and the regional tournament, largely because of her absence.

Of course, when it happened, I was devastated for her and
for the team. I could see the writing on the wall when she
went down. It was a very sad affair in our lives, especially
considering all the time she had dedicated to the sport during
the previous 13 years. But I will never forget what she said to
me in the hospital that night when she was waiting to get her
leg casted. She looked at me across the room with a smile on
her face and said, "Dad, you've got to stay happy through this
thing. Obviously God knew this was going to happen and he
has a reason for it, even though we may never know what it
is." Wow! Was I ever humbled. But I shouldn't have been
surprised. That is the way she has attacked everything in her
life: with joyful faith.

And in the same fashion she attacked her new role for the
rest of the season with incredible aggression and joy. She led
the cheering on the bench with the same passion with which
she would attack a full court press. She inspired me to be
better. She inspired me to have greater faith. That's what we
can do to each other and to the world. We can impact and
inspire by the power of God and our faith in him when we
refuse to fly below the radar.

People of impact are those who cling to God in simple and
unashamed faith and then go hard for him with whatever gifts
he has given them. Do not be ordinary! Do not be average! Be
creative! God has called us into his glorious kingdom and we
should be demonstrating some of that spectacular life to which
he has named us.

Eternal life is not just about longevity; eternal life is also
about a quality of life, a quality of life that can be lived right
now by all who continue to have themselves trained by God's
Word and who maintain a soft heart towards the voice of their
Creator.

Consider your own life. Many of us have had a Christian
upbringing and experienced the power of God in our lives or
in the life of our families. Resist the human temptation to
slide into the shadows. Take a step forward instead of a step

backwards. As Christians, we, of all people, should be excited and confident about creatively impacting this world with our lives and with the good news of the gospel. That is part of the picture of what it means to think like God.

Chapter 13

"The hard way is probably the right way."

*"But the gateway to life is very narrow
and the road is difficult, and only a few ever find it."*

~Matthew 7:14

I've never seen any rivers in my life that are totally straight. On canoe trips, you find yourself looking ahead to the next bend in the river, wondering what you are going to find when you get there. And what you usually find is just another bend up ahead.

Except for some man-made waterways, all rivers have one thing in common: they are all crooked. Why is that? The reason is quite simple—they follow the path of least resistance. Rivers find their way around anything that blocks their flow because they take the easy way. The same can be said for humanity in general.

Our natural mindset is to avoid adversity, escape trouble, and find the easiest way to get somewhere. The temptation to compromise or bend to worldly pressures and pleasures is great, for the human heart does not naturally hunger for hardship. And following the straight and narrow is hard.

More than one gospel writer reminds us that the path to God's kingdom is narrow and the road is difficult. Solomon refers to the right way in life as being straight (Proverbs 4:11, 26). *"The guilty walk a crooked path; the innocent travel a straight road"* (Proverbs 21:8). Godly King Josiah was praised for doing what was right in the sight of the Lord, for he *"walked in the ways of his father David and did not turn aside to the right or to the left"* (2 Chronicles 34:2 NASB). When we face a taxing trial ahead of us, there will always be undemanding paths of less resistance to the right or to the left.

When we set our will to follow Christ, we will have difficulties, for there are many obstacles impeding that straight course and the entry door is tiny. When Jesus talked about entering his kingdom, he said,

> *Go in through the narrow gate. The gate to destruction is wide, and the road that leads there is easy to follow. A lot of people go through that gate. But the gate to life is very narrow. The road that leads there is so hard to follow that only a few people find it.* (Matthew 7:13–14 CEV)

To think like God involves a clear understanding of this fact: going to hell is easy. To get there, all you need to do is follow your human instincts, join the big wide path that has a lot of people traveling it, and do what the majority of those people are doing. It's no wonder one of Jesus' listeners asked him one day, *"Lord, will only a few be saved?"* (Luke 13:23).

Any time Jesus talked about eternity, he implied that far fewer people will make it to heaven than to hell. He also implied that many will think they are going to make it to heaven, but they won't because of their evil deeds (Luke 13:24–27). And their evil deeds are a demonstration of the fact that they were never on the right path in the first place. They are just carelessly wandering down a trail of immorality, impurity, filthy talk, lust, hatred, and greed. But they have lots of company; the majority of the world is beside them, encouraging them along the way, because who wants to rock the boat and get people excited or upset by challenging their lifestyle? In fact, most people in the world don't even know they are on a path of destruction leading to eternal damnation. They are just comfortably moving along with the crowd, totally oblivious to the claims of God on their lives. They don't realize it, but they are headed for hell.

The words of Jesus are powerful and should cause us to examine our own journey. Are we on an easy or a hard road? If we are not experiencing much opposition, are we truly on the right path? To think like God leads one to conclude that the hard way is probably the right way.

Now, I am not referring to hard situations we have put ourselves in because of poor decisions or selfish acts. No, some hardships arrive in our lives because we have been dumb.

What I am talking about are hardships that involve dying to self, giving up rights that we think we deserve, faithfully doing the moral thing in the face of other delicious options, sacrificing financially to meet the needs of others before ourselves, bearing up boldly under persecution, and enduring pain without immediately crying to God for deliverance from the discomfort. These trials challenge our faith and require divine strength to persevere. The natural human response to such challenges is to search for an escape, an easy way out to stop the pain. If we find ourselves on an easy path, or if we are hunting for a trouble-free passageway, we are probably doing it wrong. If we are facing a choice between a simple and a difficult way forward, the hard way is probably the right way.

People typically do not want to hear this message. They want to be left alone, to find their own path to God, to dabble freely in their sinful habits and selfish desires. They want others to console them that they are not really that bad of a person, but in fact, they're pretty good, compared to really bad people. The world, and even much of the Christian world, now wants its preachers to tell them the good stuff only, stuff that doesn't offend anyone. This makes the ride easier.

Though written almost 2,000 years ago, the Apostle Paul correctly prophesied,

> *For a time is coming when people will no longer listen to sound and wholesome teaching. They will follow their own desires and will look for teachers who will tell them whatever their itching ears want to hear. They will reject the truth and chase after myths.* (2 Timothy 4:3–4)

People would rather follow strange myths than hear about dying to self. People would rather have their ears tickled than listen to a "no rights" speech. But the truth is still the truth. Following Jesus Christ is the only way to eternal life (John 14:6) and Jesus promises his true followers persecution (2 Timothy 3:12) and suffering (Philippians 1:29 and 1 Peter 2:21).

Christ also promised his followers a daily burden to bear:

> *If anyone would come after me, he must deny himself and take up his cross daily and follow me. For whoever wants to save his life will lose it, but whoever loses his life for me will save it. What good is it for a man to gain the whole world, and yet lose or forfeit his very self?* (Luke 9:23–25 NIV)

A cross? Losing your life? That doesn't sound like an easy road.

The question we are forced to ask ourselves is this: What are we giving up for God along the way? I mean, really giving up? If the hard way is probably the right way, where is it painful for us to obey Christ? The Christian life is not about entitlement, but rather, about sacrifice, taking up a cross, and self-denial. These things don't feel good—they hurt, they cause angst, they are annoying to our natural state.

What difficult thing are we denying ourselves today because we are followers of Jesus Christ? What natural desires are we depriving ourselves of because we are taking up

Christ's challenge to deny ourselves? How are we losing our natural lives today for Christ?

Oh, as his disciples, we do readily give up things. But are we just giving up the things that are easy?

I cannot speak for you, but let me illustrate from my own life. The Scriptures obviously command us to forgive those who hurt us and to refrain from allowing bitterness to grow up inside us and fester there. Some believers struggle deeply in this area. For some reason, I don't. It takes very little effort for me to obey this command. Please do not misunderstand me; I am not bragging. Forgiving offenders and carrying on with life seems to come easy for me. I do not struggle with exercising my trust in God in this area.

But in other areas of my life, I find that I have a far greater struggle to deny myself of my natural responses and behaviors. Take finances, for instance. I think I have a hard time trusting God for my finances. When I examine my emotions regarding financial sways, either up or down, I think I am far more consumed with building my own little self-sufficient world in this area than with trusting God for his provision of what I need.

As I mentioned in an earlier chapter, one of my sisters, who works in the ministry, has lived her entire married life simply trusting God to provide for all her family's financial needs. I am amazed at how she gives it over to God and how he provides bountifully. I have a hard time denying myself personal control over my money. I find it difficult to take up my cross and lose my life in this area.

And so that makes me wonder—are we just giving up stuff for Christ that is easy for us, feeling content that we are doing okay when, in reality, what he is really interested in is saving us from the stuff that is hard for us? Before we pat ourselves on the back too quickly, let me suggest this: perhaps our relationship with God is only as deep and real as our level of obedience in the area of our life that is our greatest struggle.

That is where faith plays its true role—in our areas of deepest struggle, deepest sacrifice, deepest pain—and without faith it is impossible to please God. When we walk by faith, we believe that God is all we need. When I truly believe, I believe that God is enough for me, that I can live without addictions, without obsessions, without faithless worry.

When Abraham took Isaac out for a walk up Mount Moriah, he was denying himself; he was taking up his cross and following after God alone. He was painfully preparing to sacrifice his most prized possession. Abraham's faith in God was so great that he was willing to go in that direction in order to be obedient, to demonstrate that God, and God alone, was sufficient for everything in his life. But it was not fun at the moment. It was agonizing and hard to walk by faith. In God's plan for Abraham's life, the hard way was the right way.

I wonder if we refuse to deny ourselves certain things because the rush of their presence in our lives is better than the rush of knowing God in complete abandonment. When we have not known God as intimately as we should, worldly things and attitudes can seem more attractive. The initial pain of self-denial and sacrifice does not seem worth it.

We are afraid to lose our lives in some areas, to give up control. We somehow think that these things that we cling to are our lifesavers when, in reality, they are anvils tied around our neck, sinking us deeper in sin. What are we clinging to? What artificial privileges have we created in our own minds? What are the things we are still convinced we are entitled to?

The right to be impatient with people that annoy us? The right to exact some form of revenge or correction? The right to worldly financial security? The right to unleash our tongue? The right to want fame? The right to nurse anger? The right to be jealous of another's possessions? The right to fight for our reputation? The right to certain inappropriate sensual pleasures? The right to maintain dysfunctional control over certain people in our lives?

To give up these rights is hard. We must repent and deny ourselves of these natural impulses. Christian repentance involves turning from sin and changing directions, even when it is extremely difficult. When we began our walk with Christ, we were happy to have a change of mind, a change of direction regarding our past sin. But to walk that narrow path to heaven involves being saved continually from the sins that are so attractive.

Besides Abraham, another one of my favourite Old Testament examples of self-denial and sacrificing rights was Jonathan. Here was a young man who was groomed from birth to be the next king of Israel. He grew up fully expecting to one day take his father's place on the throne over this great nation, with all the glorious trappings included in such a position. He knew no other scenario. It would have been solidly entrenched in his psyche and future expectations. Jonathan had every right to hope for this famous future.

Things were going along nicely. Both Jonathan and his father, Saul, were victorious on the battle field and were experiencing the blessing of God. But when Saul messed up, Jonathan was also forced to pay for it. No longer would the royal line pass down through Saul's descendants. The throne was taken away from them and given to a shepherd boy.

But if we read the story carefully, we see in Jonathan a perfect picture of dying to self. He willingly submitted to God's plan regarding David as the new king, even though it meant that all his hopes and dreams were altered. Not only did he willingly accept this whole new future, he lovingly supported David as God's new anointed. He did everything possible to protect, defend, and strengthen David on his journey to the throne. In my opinion, there is no clearer example in the Old Testament of living a life of no rights, of losing your life for God and for his purposes.

It cost Jonathan to follow God and be obedient to him. It costs to follow Christ. That is why Christ instructed us to first count the cost before deciding to follow him and be his disciple—just like a smart builder counts the cost of building a tower before he begins construction (Luke 14:28).

What is it costing us to follow Christ? If it's not costing us anything, we may want to make sure we are actually on the bus. Salvation is not just a free ride to glory. We need to deal with the hard realities of our own hearts and the hard realities of Jesus' words on discipleship costs that even include exhortations like the one recorded in Luke 14:33: *"None of you can be My disciple who does not give up all his own possessions"* (NASB). Have we worked through that verse and the implications that it has for us personally?

If we are feeling that it is not that hard for us to follow Christ, we may want to ask ourselves: Is the bar high enough in my life? Have I perhaps dropped the bar so low that I am clearing it with very little effort? Let me put it this way—it can't be easy or else Jesus was lying. If it is easy, we need to examine our lives to determine if we are only submitting in the areas that are effortless for us. Taking up our cross daily in *every* area of our lives is challenging, even excruciating—like death on a cross.

And so I ask again: What are we giving up for God? Where is it painful for us to obey Christ? What difficult thing are we denying ourselves today because we are followers of Jesus Christ? What natural desire are we depriving ourselves of because we are taking up Christ's challenge to deny ourselves? How are we losing our lives today for Christ?

If we feel like being a Christian is not costing us much, we need to get more realistic about what needs to be tended to in our hearts. And the best way to do that is to get closer to our holy heavenly Father so the light of his glory will illuminate the dark recesses of sin in our hearts and we will feel the burn of conviction to listen, obey, and deny ourselves of what we have presumed are our natural rights. If we are not losing our life for Christ in some fashion today, we will lose it all in eternity.

The true way to God is hard. Following Christ with our whole heart in any environment is a challenge. Most people pick the broad way because it is easy. What they don't realize is that its course never brings any lasting satisfaction and it leads its travellers into an eternity of separation from God, into hell. And that is why to think like God leads us to a simple yet profound conclusion: the hard way is probably the right way.

Chapter 14

"Sex is one of my best gifts: Handle with care."

*"You have made my heart beat faster
with a single glance of your eyes."*

~Song of Solomon 4:9 NASB

A s the Creator and sustainer of all life, God is the author and sustainer of human sexuality. Any ethereal joy or sensual elation experienced from the act of physical union is a gift from God, probably one of his best. Apart from Jesus holding all of creation together (Colossians 1:17), there would be no human ability to think, breathe, digest, feel emotions, or enjoy sex.

Sex is God's idea. He doesn't blush when we talk about it. He is not embarrassed by its intricacies, nor does he want his creatures to be. Naturally, discretion is always prudent when discussing topics involving sexuality, but when the audience and the context are appropriate, there is only room for truth on this matter.

Christians need to get over their taboos regarding sex. Instead of the church leading the way in celebrating the glorious truths of this good and perfect gift that has come down from above (James 1:17), we have left this task to the world, and they have done a rotten job of it.

In an attempt to curb the influence of worldliness on their youth, conservative Christian churches in the past have focused on the functional procreative purpose of sex so as not to draw unnecessary attention to its alluring physical delights. But from the beginning, because woman was created out of man, the divine plan for their union involved cleaving and embracing, not just familial cohabitation; God intended, and still intends, that the two become one flesh (Genesis 2:24).

One cannot read the Song of Solomon without concluding that God endorses human sexual pleasure in the context of marriage. The characters in this divinely inspired story are having a very good time. And it doesn't take a medical degree or a master's degree in Human Physiology to conclude that sex was intended for pleasure.

But the most tragic aspect of disrespecting this precious gift from God is the hurtful consequences of its abuse. Far too many teenagers begin their sexual odyssey prematurely, without a proper understanding of the sacred nature of this gift. Sex is viewed more as sport or recreation than as a mystical union of two people. There is next to no comprehension of the bonding power of sex, especially for young girls.

Countless adolescent girls give up their virginity under the premise and promise of love, only to find out that their hearts are quickly broken and their souls are now connected deeply to someone that does not even care about them. What was intended for lifelong pleasure quickly becomes the source of regret, remorse, and deep angst. Middle schools and high schools are full of girls who have experienced that horrid transformation from innocent, vibrant pre-pubescence to stained, morose adolescence because of their premature dabbling in God's marriage gift.

But as potently damaging as sex can be outside of marriage, it is exponentially more powerful for good within a healthy marriage. When God said that the man and woman would be one flesh, he was not kidding. God doesn't do anything haphazardly, sloppily, or thoughtlessly. Sex works. When there is faithfulness, goodness, and kindness on every other level of the relationship, sexual intercourse melds two hearts and souls into something beautiful beyond words. When a wife is able to fully trust her husband and make herself completely vulnerable to him, and when a husband tenderly, thoughtfully, and sacrificially loves his wife as Christ loves the church, their sexual experiences can erase hurt, infuse health, and inspire hope.

God intended sex to be a myriad of metaphors within marital union: the glue that holds the bond strong; the oil that lubricates the machinery of understanding, compassion, and forgiveness; the fire that keeps the hearth warm with passion; the candy that hits the sweet spot of the partner. And so forth. Don't be confused—sex cannot fix a bad marriage plagued with unrepented selfishness, but in the context of two willing hearts that are tender towards God, it can be a vibrant part of that love that *"covers a multitude of sins"* (1 Peter 4:8).

I know I am beginning to sound more and more like an old fogey every day, but today's young people just do not get it. They treat sex like a decision to go to the gym for a workout. This is not a simple stop at the soda shop for a milkshake and a burger; sexuality is one of God's biggest and best gifts. God never intended his exceptional gift to be abused by casual friends who hook up just for something to do. God never intended his beautiful creation to be shamelessly exposed on the computer screens of millions of ogling addicts. I think if we listened to his voice, he might be saying, "I want to give you something so much better than what you are trying to take selfishly for yourself right now. Wait. Think about my gift to you. Handle with care."

The instructions are clear and the message is unmistakable: *"Marriage should be honored by all, and the marriage bed kept pure, for God will judge the adulterer and all the sexually immoral"* (Hebrews 13:4 NIV). God gives us this command because he knows how great the marriage bed can be for 60-plus years when it is kept pure.

Why do married people have affairs? To have better sex? I doubt it. After time, new sex becomes usual sex. No. People have affairs because they long for that deep valuable union that they once experienced with their original partner. They know the power, mystery, and ecstasy of the treasure, and so they hunt for it, even with a willingness at times to sacrifice their own children along the way.

We were meant to be obedient to God's commands and structures. When we think like him, and when we move and live within his boundaries, a rich satisfaction and peace washes over our souls. When we think like him regarding sex, this precious gift brings to us a rich storehouse of physical pleasure, psychological health, and relational unity.

But thinking like God regarding human sexuality goes far beyond physical ecstasy and spousal bonding. For, in the mind of God, there is a strong connection between human sexuality and spirituality. The New Testament refers to the church as the bride of Christ. When God wants to give us a clear picture of the relationship between Jesus and his followers, he uses the image of human marriage. The spiritual intimacy between Christ and his church is paralleled to the sexual intimacy between a man and a woman in marriage.

Even in the Old Testament, God regularly likened spiritual apostasy to sexually promiscuous behavior. The writer of 1 Chronicles spoke of a renegade Israel this way, *"But they were unfaithful to the God of their fathers and prostituted themselves to the gods of the peoples of the land, whom God had destroyed before them"* (1 Chronicles 5:25 NIV). Isaiah chastised Jerusalem for her spiritual decline in a similar fashion: *"See how the faithful city has become a harlot! She once was full of justice; righteousness used to dwell in her—but now murderers!"* (Isaiah 1:21 NIV).

God even commanded one of his prophets to marry a prostitute as a visual metaphor of how God experiences the pain of our spiritual unfaithfulness.

When the Lord first began speaking to Israel through Hosea, he said to him, "Go and marry a prostitute, so that some of her children will be conceived in prostitution. This will illustrate how Israel has acted like a prostitute by turning against the Lord and worshiping other gods." (Hosea 1:2)

When someone's heart grows cold towards God and he or she wanders away, searching for substitute sources of meaning and significance apart from the Creator, a serious situation is developing. God desires to have intimate fellowship with all of his creation; when the previously faithful believer leaves the faith, it is like a wife leaving her husband to go have sex with another man.

I do not think we will ever be able to fully understand the elaborate connection between our sexuality and our spirituality, but it is obvious that sexual behavior penetrates deep into the human soul. One cannot mess around in this area without paying a steep price—physically, psychologically, and spiritually.

As usual, independent human thinking apart from God creates far greater problems than it can solve. To think differently than God on this subject sets one on a course for ruin. The cry for, and subsequent drift towards, greater sexual freedom over the past half a century has ironically created all sorts of bondage. As the devil and his worldly system have tricked more and more victims into mishandling God's gift of sex in the name of "free love" or "individual choice and self-expression," the prison just keeps getting fuller—victims, abusers, porn-addicts, jaded marriage partners, NAMBLA members.

There are probably more people in some form of sexual bondage today than ever before in human history. Our sex-laden internet will make sure of that. Certainly, today's children are empowered to speak out against sexual abuse more readily than in decades past, but billions of pornographic images are fueling more potential predators now than at any time in history.

And we cannot underestimate the gravity of sexual sin. Some Christians are inclined to assert "sin is sin," implying that God does not view one sin as more serious than another. These believers need to read 1 Corinthians 6:9–20 again.

Don't fool yourselves. Those who indulge in sexual sin . . . or commit adultery, or are male prostitutes, or practice homosexuality . . . none of these will inherit the Kingdom of God . . . But you can't say that our bodies were made for sexual immorality. They were made for the Lord, and the Lord cares about our bodies . . . Don't you realize that your bodies are actually parts of Christ? Should a man take his body, which is part of Christ, and join it to a prostitute? Never! And don't you realize that if a man joins himself to a prostitute, he becomes one body with her? For the Scriptures say, "The two are united into one." But the person who is joined to the Lord is one spirit with him. Run from sexual sin! No other sin so clearly affects the body as this one does. For sexual immorality is a sin against your own body. Don't you realize that your body is the temple of the Holy Spirit, who lives in you and was given to you by God? You do not belong to yourself, for God bought you with a high price. So you must honor God with your body.

Sexual sins exact huge costs at every level: broken marriages, abandoned children, destroyed reputations, vanquished self-images, wasted time, and the obvious one—STDs by the bucket load. And, of course, there are no words that can fully explain what happens to a child who is sexually violated, especially by a trusted loved one. Often, men who are very nice in other aspects of their lives turn into wretched monsters as they selfishly steal their daughter's or niece's most precious possession and replace it with a new gift—wretched, unspeakable memories that will haunt their hearts, minds, and dreams until the day they die.

As well, one can only imagine the psychological damage wrought upon the practitioners of all the twisted expressions of sexuality that have risen up from the dark recesses of the human heart. How can one remain unscarred after participating in, or even viewing, sexual acts that involve animals, torture, and defecation? The internet provides innumerable grotesque expressions of sexual deviance, which cannot even be spoken of for fear of lending some semblance of credibility to their existence.

We must not be deceived by our own false ideas or by the media—the number one sex organ in your body is your conscience, and condoms do not protect the conscience. Repetitive disobedience to God can sear our conscience, and a ruined conscience is the worst depriver of sexual enjoyment. Many young people unknowingly but idiotically damage their primary sex organ before they even get married.

Why are there so many extreme sexual perversions today? People have messed up their consciences so badly that they are forced to search for more extreme experiences, trying to get some new thrill out of an act that has too quickly become jaded, defiled, spoiled, and worn out prematurely by disobedience to God.

But even if we are doing it right and living within the sexual boundaries established by God as written in his Word, there is still the danger of sex becoming too important in our lives. To think godly and properly about this subject does not mean we should be thinking about it all the time. Sex can easily become an idol in the life of a saint making a decent effort to live well. In the lives of many unbelievers, this idolatry is most certainly a given.

In Romans 1, the Apostle Paul describes a descent into sin that starts with the failure of man to give thanks to God for what he has given. Such a path inevitably includes worshipping the creation instead of the Creator (Romans 1:25). Sexual preoccupations and obsessions are clear examples of worshiping the creation instead of the Creator. Our society is definitely ripe with the worship of sex. Tabloids tease us with their scintillating stories and photos of beautiful people. Television lures us into tales of sex and scandal that whet our natural sinful appetites. Movies create worlds and worldviews that make sexual preoccupation the norm. The internet fuels fantasies so far from reality, all rational thought on the subject can completely evaporate. Like oblivious children wearing no sunscreen on a hot summer afternoon, an unthankful creation recklessly splashes around in the cesspool of defiled sexuality, unknowingly awaiting the painful price to be paid for disregarding God's instructions.

On the other hand, a properly grateful heart looks at God's gift of sex with appreciation, reverence, and respect. Thankfulness leads more readily to obedience, contentment, and a commitment to holiness as expressions of love for a gracious God who has been so good to his creatures.

Thinking like God involves an understanding of sex as a gift from him to be enjoyed within its intended parameters. It is no different than any other created thing that has a purpose. Take a hammer, for instance; this heavy steel tool is most efficient when used as intended—for driving in nails. However, it becomes totally destructive when used for purposes not intended by its creator: picking your teeth, scything wheat, or writing on a chalk board.

Sex is intended for pleasure and procreation within marriage. It is an incredibly powerful and effectual aspect of keeping a healthy marriage strong. It is exceedingly destructive when ventured upon without the owner's manual. Sadly, the abused often chase sexual experience as a panacea for their psychological confusion or gaping loneliness. The twisted become more twisted as they try to satisfy an insatiable, abyss-like appetite of sexual arousal and release. Those who operate outside of God's parameters in this area find themselves on a never-ending merry-go-round of proffered hope and habitual despair as each new sexual experience satisfies less than the last one.

When his six-year-old boy wants to drive Daddy's car, a loving father says, "Wait. I'll teach you how to drive; I might even help you buy your first car. You will enjoy driving, my son, but at the right time and in the right context. You will enjoy the gifts I give you and you will be far safer and experience far more joy if you wait and do it my way."

Our loving heavenly Father has a similar message for us today. He wants us to know that sex is one of his best gifts: handle with care.

.

Chapter 15

"I really don't mind body modification."

"God created human beings; he created them godlike,
reflecting God's nature."

~Genesis 1:27 MSG

Since the 1960's, the younger generations within western civilization have driven the course of its culture. Philosophies and priorities now seem to be determined more by those under thirty than those over. And one of the priorities of youth today is the notion of individual self-expression.

Many people, but especially the younger generations, are convinced that one of the most crucial aspects of becoming a human being of any value is the ability to freely express your own individuality. This individuality is most often manifested through personalized expressions of hairstyle, lifestyle, dress, speech, and/or body modification.

Human thinking at this point in history values self-expression over conformity. Since the 1960's, conformity has become depicted as a ridiculous notion of the past, where everyone brainlessly did what their elders expected them to do. Conformity now carries with it the stigma of weakness, of caving in to outside pressures that stifle personal creativity. What does God really think of all this? What value is there in being a unique individual? We are made in the image of God. We reflect his nature. Though he is holy and transcendent, we can still see some of his characteristics when we look in the mirror. Like God, we can think, reason, love, and experience emotions. We have the freedom to choose and make decisions. Like him, we possess self-consciousness, the capacity for moral reflection, and the ability to rule over other creatures. But being made in the image of God also means that we possess the ability to create.

God was passionate about his creation—he admired his work each step of the way. Artists, architects, and builders love to create and love to admire what they create. To be truly creative can be an expression of godlikeness. In fact, we probably dishonor our Creator when we are bland and boring. Just because a song has the word Jesus in it doesn't necessarily make it good music, especially if there is nothing creative about its composition.

So, as a starting point, creative self-expression can be seen as a good thing. When humans, out of their inner souls, passionately create art and personal images that are new and fresh, ones that do not violate principles of purity and goodness, a god-like activity is occurring. Being creative within a context of sensitivity towards the heart of God reflects his nature. It is fair to say that God was expressing himself as he created the universe and everything in it. Likely, he enjoyed the process.

But as noble as creativity may be, conformity also has its value. Think of the blessings of conformity, the act of mimicking the behavior of someone else. Consider what it does for us. Conformity gives us necessary structure and predictability in our society. We live in community. Generally, we all eat the same condiments on our hamburgers as opposed to cherry pie filling. Generally, we all wear our pants on the lower part of our bodies and our shirts on the top. We all agree that going to the bathroom *in* the bathroom is the most desirable choice. Conformity is not all bad.

Neither is all self-expression automatically good. I don't think anyone would celebrate the individuality of someone next to them on an airplane who decided a week earlier to stop showering and using deodorant. Just because someone boldly declares, "I need to be able to express my individuality!" doesn't mean that the outcome will bring any lasting value or pleasure to anyone else.

The concept of self-expression needs careful scrutiny. It may be possible that many of our acts of individual self-expression are not manifestations of individualism at all. Some people like to think of themselves as unique individuals who are courageously resisting societal pressure to place them in a particular mold. But in reality, they may be behaving as conformists who are subjecting themselves to more worldly pressure than they realize.

People make attempts to be different, but as they try something "new" they are often merely conforming to the next fad that is emerging. For instance, in the twenty-first century, does anyone truly believe that getting a tattoo or a piercing carries with it even a hint of individuality? Is not this behavior simply an act of compliance to the latest sub-culture, the latest media-endorsed MTV fashion craze?

Tattoos and piercings are not morally right or wrong in themselves. In fact, according to the Old Testament, slaves in Hebrew culture who grew to love their owners during their initial six years of service would pierce their earlobe as a symbol of lifelong commitment to their master who had treated them so kindly (Exodus 21:5–6).

Sometimes too much is made of the body modification issue by Christian institutions trying to hold back a perceived flood of worldliness into their sphere of influence. When a Christian school or church has restrictions in the area of body modification, it should be based on dress code preferences as opposed to a theological justification. These matters need not have much to do with God at all. We can pierce our bodies and also love the Lord deeply. We can get a tattoo and also obey God passionately. We can even walk around in a three-piece suit with short hair and no body modifications but ignore or even disdain the glorious Lord who lovingly created us.

Body modifications or any forms of attempted self-expression are not wrong in themselves. Conformity is not necessarily right. Motive is the key concern within self-expression and conformity. Are we doing it to glorify God, or are we doing it to glorify ourselves? Are we doing it with careful and creative thought, or are we just brainlessly following a crowd of rebels or cookie cutter saints? We need to seriously consider what we desire to do—is it actually unique, or are we just being pulled along by others for no good purpose? Are our important acts of self-expression really self-expression at all?

And how important is human self-expression in God's mind anyway? Yes, God has created each of us special, with a particular gifting intended to fit into the church. In the body of Christ, we have eyes, feet, and many other body parts that function differently, but always towards the same goal. It's hard to imagine Jesus devoting a great deal of thought towards self-expression in itself. Sure, he was a unique individual, but his uniqueness flowed out of his unique standing (God in the flesh) and his unique mission (establish a heavenly kingdom and save the world). Creating a unique persona just for its own sake seems out of character with the whole counsel of God.

Besides, conformity plays a central role in the salvation of man—not a blind, mindless conformity, but a conformity with a higher purpose. Believers have been predestined to be conformed to the likeness of Christ (Romans 8:29). Obedience to his will is a common thread throughout the concept of Christian discipleship. Those who desire to be in right relationship with God are exhorted to follow Christ. As well, we are to imitate God (Ephesians 5:1), Christ (1 Thessalonians 1:6), and Christian leaders (1 Corinthians 4:16; Hebrews 13:7), as well as other faithful believers (Hebrews 6:12) and churches who have obediently gone before us and blazed a clear path of godliness (1 Thessalonians 2:14).

Conform, obey, follow, imitate. These words go against the grain of natural human thinking. But sin is rooted in independence—independence from God. And when people think they are being wonderfully distinctive individuals by their acts of self-expression, they are, most likely, conforming to the world. That is why the biblical writers instruct us to avoid bad conformity. In Romans 12:2, the Apostle Paul warns us to not be conformed to the world but be transformed by having our minds renewed (the very purpose of this book). The Apostle Peter also writes, "*As obedient children, do not conform to the evil desires you had when you lived in ignorance. But just as he who called you is holy, so be holy in all you do*" (1 Peter 1:14–15 NIV).

As I said, the most important consideration in this matter of conformity and creative individuality is motive. The Scriptures illustrate this for us through the lives of at least two individuals: Solomon and Peter.

In the Old Testament, King Solomon was the ultimate self-expression guy. Living 3,000 years ago, he was not content with merely conforming to his dutiful and proper role as king of Israel. He wanted to express his individuality and find meaning in every possible avenue that his tremendous wealth could buy.

Solomon was rich beyond our imagination. And he used his money and leisure time to express his individuality in countless areas: in philosophical discussions, in alcohol experimentation, in building multiple unique houses, vineyards, personalized gardens, parks, and even his own personalized forests irrigated by his own man-made ponds. He collected a unique array of slaves and animal flocks that could be rivaled by no one. Everything he possessed was bigger and better than had ever preceded him. He was a writer, so he expressed himself in many poems and proverbs and he hired the best singers to sing his creative works. He even attempted forms of sexual self-expression that blew the doors off of any conformist standard—he took 1,000 women into his sexual domain. If body modification had been a part of his culture, I am sure he would have lavished himself in that area as well, attempting to experience every possible form of meaningful individualistic self-expression.

And after this rich and powerful man had experimented with every possible and available form of self-expression, he writes in Ecclesiastes 2:10–11,

> *Anything I wanted, I would take. I denied myself no pleasure. I even found great pleasure in hard work, a reward for all my labors. But as I looked at everything I had worked so hard to accomplish, it was all so meaningless— like chasing the wind. There was nothing really worthwhile anywhere.*

Solomon's situation afforded him every possible form of unique self-expression, but it did not meet the need of his heart because he was doing it for the wrong motive. He was the ultimate unique individual but he felt gross and empty. "*I hated life,*" he said (Ecclesiastes 2:17 NASB). He was executing this behavior to find meaning in the acts themselves. Ultimately, he was doing them to glorify himself rather than to glorify God. And that is why he was totally frustrated in the end—chasing wind, worthless.

But consider another biblical character, this time in the New Testament. The Apostle Peter was a very unique individual, a master of self-expression who lived his life to glorify God instead of himself. Peter was far from perfect, but as he flailed along amidst his triumphs and failures, he always seemed to be endeavoring to bring glory to God and to the building of his kingdom.

And all the while he behaved uniquely, he was in the process of conforming himself to the image of Christ, a fairly important concept in the mind of God. Peter didn't put on a show to shine a spotlight on himself or make decisions based on the sole premise of being different. He wanted to follow his master with every creative ounce of gusto within his bones.

Throughout his energetic and boisterous life, Peter did a lot of things first, before others dared to jump in. For instance, he was the first disciple to follow Jesus (along with his brother, Andrew), the first to be made a fisher of men. Jesus called him to follow, and before anyone else responded, Peter said, "I'm in." Peter was always the first to respond to the Lord. He was the first to proclaim the deity of Christ, that Jesus was God. When Jesus asked his disciples, "Who do men say that I am?" Peter replied, *"You are the Christ, the son of the living God"* (Matthew 16:16 NASB).

One night, the disciples were in a boat out on the Sea of Galilee and a storm arose quickly, threatening to take their lives. Jesus came to them, walking on the water. And what did Peter do? He said, *"Lord if it's you . . . tell me to come to you on the water"* (Matthew 14:28 NIV). Jesus invited him to come, and Peter walked on the water. He jumped right out of the boat and went to Jesus, regardless of what the other disciples were going to do.

At another point in the ministry of Christ, the less dedicated, more peripheral followers of Jesus started to drift away when the teachings and challenges became more difficult. So Jesus asked if his twelve close disciples would desert him also. Peter responded by saying, *"Lord, to whom shall we go? You have the words of eternal life. We believe and know that you are the Holy One of God"* (John 6:68–69 NIV).

As the crucifixion was drawing near, Peter was the first to promise to never desert Jesus, no matter what the others did (Matthew 26:33). And though he was the first to deny the Lord three times, he was also the first to defend him with a sword in the Garden of Gethsemane (John 18:10–11). After the resurrection, Peter was the first to enter the empty tomb and, consequently, the first one of the disciples to whom Jesus appeared after his resurrection (Luke 24:34).

So it's not surprising to see that, in the first twelve chapters of the book of Acts, Peter is the spokesman for the early church at Jerusalem. On the Day of Pentecost, when people questioned if the disciples were drunk because they were speaking in tongues, Peter was the first to respond; he preached a sermon that aroused the hearts of 3,000 people to surrender to Christ.

Later, when there was a church debate over whether Gentiles could become Christians without first having to become Jews, he was the first to speak up for the Gentiles before the Council of Jerusalem based on the vision that God had given him, showing that everyone was now free to come to Christ for the forgiveness of their sins (Acts 15).

Even in his death, Peter wanted to do things in a unique manner. When Emperor Nero had him sentenced to death, tradition tells us that Peter insisted on being crucified upside down—not to draw attention to himself but because he did not feel worthy to be killed in the same manner as his Lord.

Clearly, he was far from pristine, but in Peter we see someone who was a true individual, a champion of self-expression. Yes, his rough edges needed to be smoothed out by the Holy Spirit, but he always sought to glorify God through his self-expression.

And that is the challenge to which we are called today as well. This is not about self-expression or conformity being innately right or wrong. Again, it is about motives. Our actions are right or wrong depending on why we are behaving in that manner. Even Peter messed up one time with a conformity issue. He was hanging out with some non-Jewish church folks in the city of Galatia when some big-wig Jewish dignitaries from Jerusalem showed up. As soon as they arrived, Peter started conforming to the old Jewish customs; he even stopped eating with his Gentile friends because he was afraid of what the Jewish leaders would think. For this behavior, he had to be rebuked by the Apostle Paul (Galatians 2:11–14).

On this occasion, Peter fell into a conformity trap that was based on negative peer pressure . . . and this was wrong. But thankfully, most of Peter's life was spent being different than his peers and different than those in his culture around him. And that difference was based on a genuine motive of creating a unique life of obedience to his Maker and Redeemer. This is an interesting combination of conformity and individualism, all wrapped up in one package.

Do we really want to be different? We should try visiting someone we do not know in an old folks home. Do we really want to be different? Maybe we should give away more food than we consume for one week. Do we really want to be different? Perhaps we should try spending more money on another person's survival than on our own entertainment. Do we really want to be different? Then consistently replace reality TV with reality. Do we really want to be different? Then we need to let the shadow of the cross leave its mark on our every action, thought and attitude, not just on a few inches of our skin with a tattoo. There are hundreds of God-honoring ways for Christians to be truly different if we just think about it.

God is saying today, "I really don't mind body modification. That's not the point." To think like God on this matter involves deep examination of our motives. Are we glorifying ourselves or are we glorifying God? If you have a sincere desire to be an individual, if you truly want to be unique, if you want to glorify God, then do something radical for his honor as you conform to his glorious image!

Chapter 16

"Some thanks would be nice."

*"Let every detail of your lives—words, actions, whatever—
be done in the name of the Master, Jesus,
thanking God the Father every step of the way."*

~Colossians 3:17 MSG

Ingratitude is one of the most repulsive of all possible human qualities. We are not surprised by its presence in young children, but we work hard to massage it out of them. We are frustrated by its lingering presence in adolescence and disgusted by its existence in adults we meet.

If we are annoyed by a lack of thankfulness, imagine how it grieves God, the giver of all life. I know that I have given gifts in the past and then anxiously waited for the appropriate response of gratitude, only to be disappointed. It is frustrating to have efforts of sacrifice go unnoticed, unappreciated. It is vexing to be taken for granted. If God were more human, he would exist in a continual state of immeasurable angst, pointlessly waiting for his creation to show its appreciation for his ongoing goodness.

But he is not like us, and he encourages us to be more like him in his graciousness.

*Love your enemies! Do good to them. Lend to them without
expecting to be repaid. Then your reward from heaven will
be very great, and you will truly be acting as children of the
Most High, for he is kind to those who are unthankful and
wicked.* (Luke 6:35)

Even though, in his mercy, God is kind to unthankful
people, some thanks would be nice.
It is human to take things for granted, to be presumptuous.
It is godlike to be thankful. Human thinking is forgetful,
regularly missing the obvious. During moments of profound
pensiveness, we come to the conclusion that we must be
thankful to God for his bountiful blessings. It is the obvious
answer. Any other is quite absurd. So, during one weekend
each fall, we are particularly vigilant to do our proper duty.
But what does appropriate human gratitude look like in the
mind of God? Certainly, it is of critical importance. Isaiah
says it is the job of the living to give thanks to God (Isaiah
38:19). Christ retained his thankful attitude through the home
stretch of his walk to the cross (1 Corinthians 11:24). Godly
men like the Apostle Paul could not stop talking about it. At
least fifty verses in his epistles include an exhortation or
allusion to thankfulness. One brief section in Colossians alone
includes three references to it (3:15–17).
Another passage in Romans connects unthankfulness to a
resulting human stupidity that leads to idolatry and then, inevitably, to a tragic spiraling into deeper and deeper sin (1:21–32).

*For even though they knew God, they did not honor him as
God, or give thanks, but they became futile in their
speculations, and their foolish heart was darkened.
Professing to be wise, they became fools, and exchanged the
glory of the incorruptible God for an image in the form of
corruptible man and of birds and four footed animals and
crawling creatures. Therefore, God gave them over in the
lusts of their hearts to impurity . . .* (Romans 1:21–24
NASB)

And again, later in the same passage,

Just as they did not see fit to acknowledge God any longer,
God gave them over to a depraved mind, to do those things
that are not proper. (1:28 NASB)

Ingratitude towards God can be a sure recipe for disaster.
Failing to acknowledge him rightly and forgetting to thank
him for his provisions can lead to a depraved mind that is
capable of all sorts of standard and sordid sin. Check out the
list for yourself. The litany of horrid behaviors recorded in the
second half of Romans chapter 1 appears to be attributed to a
failure to give thanks to the Creator, a failure to properly
respect and respond to his eternal power and divine nature
(Romans 1:20).

We think we are a thankful people, but much of our
gratitude is ritualistic. We breathe a quick "Thank you, Lord!"
after we pass a tough exam, much like "Gesundheit!" after a
sneeze. In our culture, "Thanks" can be merely a polite
response, akin to saying "Sorry" when we bump into someone
inadvertently in a crowded hallway.

In our pop culture we see it regularly. Professional
athletes, especially football players, seem to be very grateful
to God when they make a big play on the field. But sadly, we
hear the equally common, yet mocking "Thank you, Jesus!"
uttered by scoffers and pagans who jest about a subject they
do not understand.

We hear and use the words readily, but how often and how
deeply are we truly grateful to God? What does genuine
gratitude look like? Living in the wealthiest nations of the
earth does not help matters for us.

It is hard to be earnestly thankful amidst affluence. The
continual presence of abundance inoculates our minds,
causing them to become less responsive. Our perceptions start
to twist. Hopes become expectations. Dreams become
demands. We become used to having what we need and,
largely, even what we want. We become disgusting.

Most likely, we are never sincerely thankful until we have had to do without. There is no substitute for deprivation as the master teacher of gratitude. When we must live without something important or critical for any extended period of time, we learn to appreciate things that should not be taken for granted: a great meal after not eating all day, a hot shower after being in the cool, damp woods for a week.

And so, amidst plenty and busyness, we need to find a way to not forget. At times, we may even need to force ourselves to be thankful. Perhaps that is what the Psalmist meant by his encouragement for believers to *"Offer to God a sacrifice of thanksgiving"* (Psalm 50:14 NASB). Sometimes it takes effort. It does not come naturally.

Murmuring, grumbling, complaining—these come naturally. Human nature sees the glass half empty before it notices it's half full. The children of Israel jumped into this whining game as soon as they faced the trials associated with their deliverance from Egypt. Instead of thanking God for their redemption out of slavery and from the house of bondage (Joshua 24:17), they were upset with God and with his servant Moses. They quickly forgot the horrors of their past oppression, claiming that they wanted to go back to Egypt rather than face the challenges of the new day. Instead of thanking God for the gift of manna in the wilderness, they grumbled for meat.

But we are no better than the Israelites, even though we have read their story and hopefully learned something from it. We do not appreciate what we have. We want more. We are jealous. Even if we own a nice home or car, we are envious of our neighbor who has a nicer one. We do not see the thousands of good gifts God gives us every day. We do not thank him appropriately for every breath, even though we know it is him giving it to us (Daniel 5:23). We forget the good things he gave us last week: the answers to prayer, the deliverances from temptation and danger. We forget where we would be without his salvation. We fail to appreciate how sinfully ugly our lives would be without his saving grace.

To live in sync with the mind and heart of God involves cultivating an attitude and lifestyle of thankfulness. This is nothing short of radical. Such a lifestyle begins, as usual, with repentance—a change of mind about ourselves and about the grace of God that puts us in a different position than where we would be without his protective hand.

Again, we are so arrogant. We assume that we are in the place we find ourselves because of our own doing. We presume that our children are doing well solely because of the good choices that they have made. We forget the enormous role God's grace plays in the successes in our lives and in the lives of our families. Genuine thankfulness is rooted in a proper understanding of, and appreciation for, our salvation in Jesus Christ. Unless we understand where we would be without him in our lives, we will fail to be properly grateful.

And we also fail to see, and be thankful for, the grace of God that comes in the forms of hardship and disappointment. Though we should, we rarely appreciate the trials that break us, that keep us humble, that keep our wandering hearts tethered to the Savior. We need a paradigm of gratitude that appreciates the good and bad circumstances that arrive at our door. To develop this worldview requires faith in God and in his goodness. It requires a belief that whatever is going on in our lives at this time is from the hand of God—he is giving us what we need. And for this, we must be thankful.

The will of God for our lives is clear in the Scriptures: "*In everything give thanks, for this is God's will for you in Christ Jesus*" (1 Thessalonians 5:18 NASB). But we are exhorted not only to give thanks *in* all circumstances but also *for* all things. "*Always giving thanks to God the Father for everything, in the name of our Lord Jesus Christ*" (Ephesians 5:20 NIV). This is where we feel the greatness of the gap between our natural minds and the mind of God. How can we be thankful *for* everything? Does this really mean the terrible parts as well?

I think we have a paltry view of thanksgiving. I think we fail to grasp its true significance. It is interesting to note that several biblical writers give the impression that the whole point of our salvation is so that we can give thanks to the holy name of the Lord (Psalm 106:47, 1 Chronicles 16:35). So often, we wrongly convince ourselves that our salvation is all about how our lives can be improved, how we can feel better and enjoy life more fully.

Consequently, we probably do too much begging when we talk to God. Our prayers should not be wish lists or cries for deliverance from uncomfortable conditions; they should be thoughtful petitions flavored with thanksgiving (Colossians 4:2). We are told to be thankful, not anxious (Philippians 4:6–7). This is how the peace of God washes over our troubled hearts and minds amidst confusing trials. In matters of conscience where we are taking a stand in a grey area, we are told to thank God regardless of which side we take (Romans 14:6). In Ephesians 5:4 thankfulness is seen as the necessary opposite to the bad use of the tongue—filthiness, silly talk, and coarse jesting.

Paul encouraged us to thank God for our future inheritance amidst heavenly glory (Colossians 1:12). Also, we need to appreciate the people that God has put into our lives (Philemon 4–5), both those who bless us and those who challenge us. Certainly, we should thank him for the ministry opportunities he affords us (1 Timothy 1:12). Even our songs should be expressions of thankfulness to him (Psalm 28:7). And this sacrifice of praise and thanksgiving to God is something that needs to be offered up continually, not just once in a while (Hebrews 13:15).

But be careful—this has nothing to do with feeling good. It is all about being obedient, being thankful to the almighty divine Creator for everything that happens to us. Again, this is difficult and requires trust. When we give our own children what they need, be it praise or discipline, we do so because we are wisely providing the circumstances necessary to help mold them into healthy, balanced adults with spiritual and emotional maturity. When they are young, we do not expect them to be grateful to us for what we provide, but some thanks would be nice eventually, especially when they mature into adulthood.

We do not demand it of our children, but it is the right response. Of course, there are exceptions because some childhoods are horrific, but generally, full grown children who fail to appreciate the goodness and sacrifice of their parents' efforts are still immature, still falling short of the right behavior. Such ingratitude is shameful.

And our ingratitude towards God is also shameful. But it is also scary. Listen to the Psalmist Asaph who writes, *"Repent, all of you who forget me, or I will tear you apart, and no one will help you. But giving thanks is a sacrifice that truly honors me. If you keep to my path, I will reveal to you the salvation of God"* (Psalm 50:22–23). This is starting to sound like pretty serious stuff. God warns us through the Apostle Paul that one of the sure signs of the last days is the abundance of ingratitude (2 Timothy 3:2). And to the Colossian church he writes that it is on account of various sins, including greed, that the wrath of God will come upon the earth (Colossians 3:6–7). Greed and ingratitude go hand in hand. Desiring what others have, or simply desiring more, are tell-tale signs of an unthankful heart.

We are influenced by the world and its jaded, unappreciative spirit. The world's system trains its members to be presumptuous and unsatisfied with what they have. Human thinking does not naturally see the importance of perpetual gratitude. We need a renewal of our minds. We need to think like God.

Perhaps we need a glimpse into the future to be reminded of its significance right into the eternal state. In Revelation 4:9 we see the throne room in heaven and we hear the four living creatures giving *"thanks to him who sits on the throne, to him who lives forever and ever"* (NASB). In Revelation 7:12 we also hear the great multitude from every nation, clothed in white robes, giving thanks to God. And in Revelation 11:17

there is a cry of thanksgiving to God because, after what seems to be a long wait, he has finally begun to reign. As the kingdom of God comes to full fruition in the last days, thanksgiving will remain a natural part of the ongoing dialogue.

But before closing off this topic, it is crucial to remember that a proper response of gratitude goes far beyond mere words. Yes, the words are important, but they must be accompanied by actions that demonstrate the integrity of the heart. A truly thankful husband will help with the children without expecting glamorous recognition. A truly thankful child will pitch in and do his or her chores cheerfully, acknowledging Mom's hard work in the home. A truly thankful saint will walk in obedience and holiness because there is a comprehension of the grace of God and the value of forgiveness. When the richness of the gift of salvation is grasped, an active thanksgiving will flow. And it will be a pervasive attitude that colors every corner of our lives.

Perhaps someday we will even be able to respond to adversity as courageously as commentator Matthew Henry[4] did after being robbed of his wallet:

Let me be thankful first because I was never robbed before;
second, because although they took my purse, they did not
    take my life;
third, because although they took my all, it was not much;
and fourth, because it was I who was robbed, not I who
    robbed.

Some thanks would be nice.

---

[4] As viewed online at http://www.rayfowler.org/2007/11/21/matthew-henrys-thanksgiving-testimony (accessed Nov. 21, 2008).

Chapter 17

"My favorite worship is holy obedience."

"Do you think all God wants are sacrifices—empty rituals just for show? He wants you to listen to him! Plain listening is the thing, not staging a lavish religious production."

~1 Samuel 15:22 MSG

Last chapter I suggested that a thankful heart is the only suitable response to the gracious generosity of our glorious Creator. Every day, and in ways we do not even notice or comprehend, God gives good things to all of his creatures, both the just and the unjust. I also suggested that the best demonstration of gratitude on our part is our obedience to the commands of God. This idea begs expansion.

Man's respectful response to God is often referred to as worship. Worship typically includes praise, honor, and devotion towards the Almighty. The English word is rooted in worthiness. Obviously, God is worthy of all the love, reverence, and adoration we can marshal. Given the fact that he is so fantastic, so powerful, and so "other," he seems to be worthy of much more than what any frail human could muster.

How do we respond fittingly to the Maker of billions of galaxies as well as the emotions of our hearts?

God's thoughts are very clear on this matter.

True worship of God is inextricably easier and harder than we make it out to be. It's easier because it all boils down to one main idea—obedience; it's harder because deep down in our hearts we don't really want to obey.

From the outset, we must not miss the point: *"Behold, to obey is better than sacrifice"* (1 Samuel 15:22 NASB). The sacrifice is good and necessary, but our obedience is better. We must not neglect our prayers (1 Thessalonians 5:17), our tithes and offerings (Malachi 3:10), and our gathering together as believers (Hebrews 10:25). We must faithfully and lovingly do these things because God has instructed us to do so. But we cannot do these things thinking that they are the sum total of our worship. We cannot do these things and neglect obedience. And most of all, we cannot do these things as a cover-up for our deliberate disobedience.

There is no pay-off that causes God to look the other way on our behavioral compromises and missteps. We cannot bribe God into some form of acquiescence regarding our sin. In our worldly society, money and other favors grease the wheels of the machine in favor of the rich. Police services can be bought, magistrative positive discrimination can be purchased, and business deals can be lubricated by money. Not so with God. Our sacrifices, though necessary, do not buy off God in any way.

Human thinking on this matter is quite muddled. We mistakenly view our various forms of worship as part of a deal that we have with God, a transaction. We think that, in exchange for our salvation, we pay God back with acts of sacrificial worship. We attend church and maybe even get involved in some form of ministry (musical or teaching or service-oriented). We give tithes to the church as well as to other missions and relief organizations. We sing praises to his name every Sunday morning and feel emotionally connected

to him in the midst of a moving sermon. But while we do
these things, we subconsciously run a tally sheet in our brain
that totals the value of our sacrifice so that we can judge
whether or not we have done enough, whether or not we think
the bill has been paid.

That is why we become demanding of God in tough
situations. Amidst trials, we may be tempted to think that we
have been faithful in our duty and now God is somehow
letting down his end of the bargain. Because we have
devotedly done our task, he does not have the right to fail to
come through for us in the manner in which we think he
should. We feel betrayed and demand that God fix things so
we can go back to feeling better. Because we have worshiped
him so wonderfully, we may even think that he owes us
something.

These confused thoughts often rise to the fore in the area
of our worship through tithing, especially when we compare
our giving to the giving of others. Studies show that the
average Christian gives only 2% of his or her income to the
Lord.[5] When we hear this, we feel we are doing well to give
the standard 10% prescribed throughout church history. When
we give 20%, we consider ourselves to be outstanding.

So, how much should we give? The new covenant says
only that we should give liberally from a generous heart that
has experienced the generosity of God's salvation. Certainly,
the debate regarding how much we should give financially is
one that is complex and open-ended, but to lose ourselves in it
would be to miss the main point here. The main point is that
there are two main points: freely give a portion of your
money, time, and talents to God's kingdom, but do not
consider it to be any form of payment.

When our tithing is considered a payment, we are guilty of
allowing our worship to become dutiful and ritualistic. Consequently, our other forms of worship can become dutiful and

[5] Randy Alcorn, "Giving Less Than a Tithe?"
http://www.surfinthespirit.com/finances/giving.html.

ritualistic. Our church attendance can come to be considered "putting in our time" and our church ministry can come to be viewed as a compensation for our sins of the week. No, this is not an exchange policy. We are not to perform our acts of sacrificial worship as a means of making a sufficient contribution to appease God. Ultimately, he wants our obedience. There are no two ways about it.

But instead of pure and simple obedience, we rationalize and justify our behavior. That is what got King Saul into a whole heap of trouble, ultimately excluding him from continuing as king. Instead of fully obeying the instructions of the Lord to destroy everything among the Amalekites (1 Samuel 15:3), he kept alive some of the best animals *"to sacrifice to the Lord your God"* (1 Samuel 15:15 NASB). Even though Saul claimed that he changed the command of the Lord for a good reason (to perform a lovely act of worship with choice specimens), the Lord referred to his behavior as rebellion and insubordination (1 Samuel 15:23 NASB).

This is not the first time Saul behaved this way. Earlier in the story, Saul got impatient while waiting for Samuel to show up to make the burnt offering before going into battle, so he did it himself (1 Samuel 10:8 cf. 13:8–9). Even though this act had the appearance of godly worship (entreating the favor of the Lord before going to battle against his enemies), Samuel condemned him for acting foolishly and for not keeping the commandment of the Lord (1 Samuel 13:13). Saul was not in the position to perform this duty, so no rationalization would cover his sin.

To think like God on this matter is unambiguous. If we are faced with a choice of simply doing what God says or doing something else that seems like a good idea because it involves some nice worship of God, we just need to obey. His commands are not simply advice or mere suggestions. He is not offering a few tips for better living. His directives are the instructions of the righteous Creator and Judge of the living and the dead. These orders are coming from the Sustainer of all life. Do we actually think we have options?

We must be cautious. There is a tendency to think we are doing better than we really are. We are convinced that God is pleased with our worship. But what we may consider to be a sweet aroma of sacrifice might actually be stench in the nostrils of the Lord. If there is iniquity in our hearts, our repetitive and numerous offerings bring no pleasure to God—they are worthless. It's like we are making an appearance before him with insincere hearts. God hates these acts of worship; they are an abomination to him. When we are harboring sin, God refuses to listen to our prayers and literally hides himself from us.

This message is repeated throughout the Scriptures. Hosea writes, *"For I delight in loyalty rather than sacrifice, and in the knowledge of God rather than burnt offerings"* (Hosea 6:6 NASB).

Micah says,

> *How can I stand up before God and show proper respect to the high God? Should I bring an armload of offerings topped off with yearling calves? Would God be impressed with thousands of rams, with buckets and barrels of olive oil? Would he be moved if I sacrificed my firstborn child, my precious baby, to cancel my sin? But he's already made it plain how to live, what to do, what God is looking for in men and women. It's quite simple: Do what is fair and just to your neighbor, be compassionate and loyal in your love, and don't take yourself too seriously—take God seriously.* (Micah 6:6–8 MSG)

And the most precise way to take God seriously is to obey him. Jesus said, *"Blessed are those that hear the word of God, and observe it"* (Luke 11:28 NASB). But to the hypocritical religious leaders of his day he delivered this message: *"What sorrow awaits you Pharisees! For you are careful to tithe even the tiniest income from your herb gardens, but you ignore justice and the love of God. You should tithe, yes, but do not neglect the more important things"* (Luke 11:42).

There are important aspects of worship that need to be exercised (tithing, praising, singing, praying, serving, preaching, etc.), but there are even more important things that need to be addressed before we continue to play the game of dutiful worship. We need to smarten up and start heeding God—in every avenue of our lives. Any other choice is audacious and wrong. Thinking like God involves under-standing that obedience is his favorite part of worship.

And so, dear brothers and sisters, I plead with you to give your bodies to God because of all he has done for you. Let them be a living and holy sacrifice—the kind he will find acceptable. This is truly the way to worship him. (Romans 12:1).

Could it be stated any more clearly?

I am astounded by the behavior of the institutionalized church throughout history. Consider the massive and magnificent structures that have been built, presumably for the glory of God.

Between 1180 and 1270 in France alone, 80 cathedrals, 500 abbey churches, and tens of thousands of parish churches were constructed in stone; more stone was quarried for churches in medieval France than had been extracted for the Great Pyramid in ancient Egypt, which alone had consumed 40.5 million cubic feet of stone.[6]

These structures are spectacular and awe-inspiring places of worship, but they hold little eternal value if they are housing saints with cold, disobedient hearts.

Consider the elaborate religious rituals that have been crafted in the name of glorifying and worshiping God: the inauguration of popes, the launching of crusades, the crowning

---

[6] *The Encyclopedia of World History 2001*, s.v. "Western Europe and the Age of the Cathedrals, 1000–1300," http://www.bartleby.com/67/443.html (accessed November 18, 2008).

of monarchs. Historically, the church has staged big productions to reflect the significance of the activities they endorsed. Historically, the church has missed the point.

But even today, I am confounded by the time and energy we put into our religious productions. Yes, it is glorifying to God to play skillfully to his name (Psalm 33:3). Yes, we should praise him with an array of instruments (Psalm 150). Yes, if we are going to offer sacrifices of musical and speaking talents to the King of Kings, it should be done well, with thoughtful care and disciplined practice. Yes, we need to bring our best, not our lamest, offerings to God (Malachi 1:6–8). And yes, we need to bring offerings to God that are truly a sacrifice, things that actually cost us something (1 Chronicles 21:24). But I think we are amiss to believe God is as impressed with our religious shows as we are. And we are doubly amiss if we think we can perform these practices as the entirety of our worship of God or as a compensation for our disobedience.

In the mind of God, true worship is about total submission, about complete abandonment to a world of compliance to his Word. It is a living and holy manifestation of the power of God in the life of a human. This, and this demonstration alone, rises up to God as a sweet smelling aroma, completely acceptable in his sight. God is saying today, as he has said for thousands of years, "My favorite worship is holy obedience."

Chapter 18

"Invest your life,
don't just spend it."

*"Instruct them to do good, to be rich in good works, to be
generous and ready to share, storing up for themselves
the treasure of a good foundation for the future."*

~1 Timothy 6:18–19 NASB

When I was a young boy, I remember asking my father to help me understand the difference between spending and investing. In his explanation, he used the common illustration of buying a car compared to buying a house. Generally, the value of real estate appreciates over time while the value of a car depreciates, even as we drive it off the lot.

Obviously, we need to spend some of our money on things that have no chance of increasing in worth (food, clothing, transportation), but if we have no avenues of investment, we may come to a point in our lives where we have nothing. Financially, a future devoid of poverty usually requires some planning and monetary sacrifice in the earlier days of the story.

But fiscal retirement plans are only a part of the investments that beckon us throughout life. Failing to invest attention and tender care into our children's lives can leave us with poor family relationships in our declining years. The same can be said about relationships in general. If we do not invest proper time and consideration into friendships during our young adult years, we can end up very much alone and lonely when we are older.

And yet, to think of investments as being limited to RSPs, income properties, and relationships is still small human thinking. To think like God on this matter involves a broader perspective, one that takes into account our heavenly future and the kingdom of God. There are far greater things to invest in besides our little lives.

Our life is but a vapor, even if we don't believe it. My, how time flies! I have never heard elderly people complain about how long it has taken to get to their age. We are here today, and before you know it, our earthly lives are done. We must be realistic. We must ask ourselves the hard question: What will endure from our lives into eternity? We need to think more deeply about investing our lives and not just spending them.

One of the most valuable non-renewable resources we possess is time. At some point in the future, the time in each of our lives will be totally depleted. Every day we have 1,440 minutes—that's 86,400 seconds. The Bible says, on average, God gives us 70, maybe 80, years, if we are strong, before "*we fly away*" (Psalm 90:10). Obviously, many people don't even get that.

Regardless of the length of our lives, we are instructed to "*number our days*" so that we live wisely (Psalm 90:12 NASB). Rich people cannot buy more hours in the day and scientists cannot invent new energy-efficient minutes. Time allows no balances, no overdrafts. If we fail to use one day's deposit effectively, our loss cannot be recovered. We cannot hoard time to be spent another day. We get one chance to do it right and then comes a day of reckoning.

One day, Jesus told the story of a nobleman who, before going on a journey, commanded his stewards to *"do business"* with a set amount of allotted capital (Luke 19:12–13). In this case, the investment capital was about 100 days of a common man's wage. When the nobleman returned, he audited them individually to see what they had done with the money. Some of the stewards had been more successful than others in their investment. The master doled out rewards according to their success but had great wrath for the steward that had done nothing with his capital, simply hiding it in a handkerchief.

From this parable we must conclude that God expects us to use our gifts from him in a profitable way. Investing vs. spending is not even a debate. There must be some return, some growth. Proceeding through our life story with a balance of zero is considered a failure. Putting our time, energy, money, and talents solely into our own little empires will not bode well when it comes time for our own personal audit. Will we be ready for such an appraisal when we stand before our Maker? Will the verdict come down as guilty—guilty of spending our lives as opposed to investing them?

In 1 Corinthians 3, the Apostle Paul explains that Christians will not face God's judgment of wrath in the future, but rather, the judgment seat of Christ, where the quality of our deeds will be exposed. He writes,

> *Because of God's grace to me, I have laid the foundation like an expert builder. Now others are building on it. But whoever is building on this foundation must be very careful. For no one can lay any foundation other than the one we already have—Jesus Christ. Anyone who builds on that foundation may use a variety of materials—gold, silver, jewels, wood, hay, or straw. But on the judgment day, fire will reveal what kind of work each builder has done. The fire will show if a person's work has any value. If the work survives, that builder will receive a reward. But if the work is burned up, the builder will suffer great loss. The builder will be saved,*

but like someone barely escaping through a wall of flames.
(1 Corinthians 3:10–15)

I think it is fair to say that building with inferior products (wood, hay, straw) is the equivalent of spending one's life. Just as these flimsy products are vanquished by the flames, our life's accomplishments will be extinguished in a moment if they have been executed with selfishness and a dedication to the preservation of our own little domains.

On the contrary, building with gold, silver, and precious stones is the equivalent of investing one's life. When the fire of judgment is applied to these valuable commodities, they are purified and come out looking even better than when they went into the furnace. A life that is invested in the kingdom of God—into the service of others—is one that has value far into eternity. And the value increases with time.

Paul says, *"So be careful how you live. Don't live like fools, but like those who are wise. Make the most of every opportunity in these evil days"* (Ephesians 5:15–16). Another translation of this passage states it as *"redeeming the time"* (KJV). Whatever time we are given, we must understand its worth. For this reason, depth is a better measurement of a life than length. And meaningful depth of life is rooted in a mindset that focuses on eternal rather than temporal matters.

Our natural tendency is to count the days until the next exciting event in our lives. Instead, God tells us to make every day count. Daily decisions on how we use our finances, our time, our thoughts, and our abilities determine our reward in the future. We cannot live as entities unto ourselves. As Christians, we cannot forget that we have been bought with a price; we must glorify God in our bodies (1 Corinthians 6:20).

So what does it look like to think like God on this topic? What does it mean to deliberately invest our lives rather than spend them? How do we gain a worthwhile return on our daily activities, both mundane and profound, so that eternal value is banked into the kingdom of God as opposed to having nothing to show for all our labors?

Though this topic is not just about money, it is certainly a lot about money; for the use of our money is a clear reflection of our true priorities. Regardless of what comes out of our mouths, where we spend our discretionary income is an indication of our treasure house. And where we put our treasure impacts where our heart remains focused. That is why Jesus encouraged his followers to not be afraid to sell all their possessions and to give the money to charity. Jesus said this would create for us *"an unfailing treasure in heaven"* (Luke 12:32–35 NASB).

Jesus' recipe for a safe investment is recorded in Matthew's gospel as well:

> *Don't store up treasures here on earth, where moths eat them and rust destroys them, and where thieves break in and steal. Store your treasures in heaven, where moths and rust cannot destroy, and thieves do not break in and steal.* (Matthew 6:19–20)

On another occasion, Christ told the parable of the wealthy farmer who built bigger and bigger barns to house the bountiful crops he had produced for his own personal consumption. The farmer said to himself, *"'You have plenty of good things laid up for many years. Take life easy; eat, drink and be merry.' But God said to him, 'You fool! This very night your life will be demanded from you. Then who will get what you have prepared for yourself?'"* (Luke 12:19–20 NIV). Jesus' closing remark about this situation is particularly powerful: *"This is how it will be with anyone who stores up things for himself but is not rich toward God"* (Luke 12:21 NIV).

Selfishness seems to be a common theme involved in the spending of a life as opposed to investing it. A great deal of effort may have been exerted, but when the dust settles, a self-centered existence leaves an empty portfolio for the future. To be rich toward God always involves thinking beyond ourselves. It also involves wrestling through challenging topics like dying to self, forgiving tremendous hurts, and loving the unlovely.

But let's be honest. There are no two ways about it—being rich toward God is probably easier for a poor person because he or she faces less temptation to drift into self-sufficiency and pride. So, why do we envy the rich, especially when we know that Jesus said it is so much harder for a rich person to enter the kingdom of God (Luke 18:24)? The rich young ruler of Jesus' day walked away sad; he could not bring himself to give up his riches to be with Jesus. We need to clean out our silly human thinking regarding the false security of riches and invest as much of our income as possible into the work of the Lord. We need to send a lot of it on up ahead.

But what else does it look like to invest our lives besides making proper monetary decisions? Here's a suggestion: the easiest way to determine if a particular behavior is an act of spending or investing is to envision any potential long term benefit to the kingdom of God. Using this criterion, it would be wise to consider most television viewing as an act of spending rather than investing. So might be a lot of our internet activities, as would be the reading of copious romance novels and an all-consuming preoccupation with sports.

A life of spending can feel intoxicating for a while, but eventually, we cannot help but be jaded by the numbing effects of self-interest. Instead of getting lost in these egocentric routines of life, we need to create more ways to perform generous acts of good works for others. Obviously, sinful habits that consume volumes of energy and time have no value in God's kingdom. And since human souls will last longer than any material item, loving people more than things will always be a safe step in the right direction.

But another criterion would be the attitude with which we execute our actions. Sometimes the attitude is more impacting than the act itself. Christian service done with evil motives would have to be considered wood, hay, and straw—a life spent and burned up. On the other hand, a professional athlete honing and practicing his craft altruistically as unto the Lord (Colossians 3:23) is a valuable investment. Adorning our lives with a spirit of forgiveness, a servant's heart, and a covering of agape love will go a long ways towards building a meaningful investment into the kingdom of God. Attitude is huge. Giving cheerfully is an entirely different enterprise than doing so grudgingly. And living life generously can mean a lot more than just being free with your cash.

Having said these things, we cannot underestimate the precious eternal value of giving our testimony to the people God brings into our path day in and day out. We must speak unashamedly of Jesus and what he has done for us. The Savior of the world must be glorified in our lives, but he must also be magnified and clarified in our speech.

There is no greater investment than giving and living the message of salvation. Being a friendly person at work and even hanging out with your unsaved colleagues are nice gestures, but if we are unwilling to share with them the gospel message of Jesus Christ specifically, how can we believe there is any lasting value to our efforts exerted?

Human thinking is naturally selfish. Humans, unsurprisingly, hoard. It takes very little effort to spend our lives on ourselves—we can do that without even trying. A human world-view consciously and subconsciously limits itself to this world and what can be accumulated in it.

God-like thinking, however, sees this world and our time here in its proper perspective. God-like thinking sees a human life as a brief moment in time but a human soul as an eternal jewel. God-like thinking sees the kingdom of God as the only thing that really matters.

Every day, business investors pick stocks in the equities markets, commodities in the futures market, and currencies in the foreign exchange in order to build fortunes that will not last. Thinking like God will give us the ability to pick the best investments possible for the best payoff in the future—the only one that will truly matter. Are we investing our lives or just spending them?

Chapter 19

"You need help;
I never intended for you
to do it alone."

*"If one person falls, the other can reach out and help.
But someone who falls alone is in real trouble."*

~Ecclesiastes 4:10

In the summer of 2005, my little town of residence experienced a torrential downpour that flooded my basement. The rainwater drained furiously into two window wells on the back side of my house and leaked in through the windows from there. For the next few days, I was vacuuming water, rearranging furniture, and dragging carpets outside to be dried in the warm summer air. It was a lot of work, but the clean-up mission was a success.

Then, just when the rugs were finally dried and returned to the basement, another serious storm started to threaten from the skies. But I was not worried. With my Shop Vac in hand and the carpet still rolled up on the opposite side of the room, I was ready to deal with any incoming water that would try to penetrate my castle . . . or so I thought.

The rain started to pound, even more fiercely than the storm four days earlier. One window well started to fill up and the water began to trickle down the wall, so I attacked the villain with the vacuum nozzle. But as I proudly stayed on top of the infiltration speed of the incoming fluid, I heard the sound of a waterfall behind me. It was the other window; the window well was totally full and the water was literally pouring in.

I assailed the new invader with my Shop Vac but quickly realized that I was losing the battle. I couldn't keep ahead of the flow. It was coming in faster than I could suck it up. As I saw the water on the concrete floor now creeping towards the freshly dried carpet, I started to yell for help. My eldest daughter was the first to arrive on the scene. She dragged the carpet further away from the approaching tide, but I knew I was not going to win the battle against the two waterfalls now cascading down my basement wall.

I yelled for more help and my wife arrived. We quickly decided our best chance for victory was to have the ladies go outside and bail the water out of the window wells while I continued to vacuum inside. It was quite a sight. I was furiously orchestrating the vacuum hose like Beethoven's baton, and my wife and daughter, like two soaked rats in the middle of a pounding monsoon, were feverishly bailing water with all their might.

Well, as the ladies got the water level down below the window ledges and the rain began to let up, we were able to turn the tide on the flood. I was able to suck up the last of the intruding rainfall so the carpet and basement were saved. We had won. We emerged victorious over the impending disaster. During the next few weeks, some new landscaping in the back yard corrected my poor runoff issues, but the lessons learned from that experience still linger with me today.

I have often thought about that experience and mused about the way I was able to gain victory over the assaulting flood waters. And the obvious conclusion that continues to ring through my memory is that I was triumphant because I did not do it alone. The only way victory came that night was with the help of others. That we need each other is not a spectacularly profound truth, but it is often a forgotten one, especially in the spiritual realm. To understand the mind of God involves grasping the truth that our Creator never intended for us to make it alone.

For various reasons and through various seasons of our lives, we gravitate to island thinking. We try to make it alone. We believe we can be self-sufficient. Sometimes our motives for retreating to "I-land" are selfish—we don't want to be bothered by others or God. We want to be free from the constraints and inhibitions that tend to accompany living in a community. And we want to do whatever we like without having to be accountable to others or needing to think about how our behavior might impact those around us.

At other times, however, we may retreat to I-land because we have been hurt or disillusioned by people. After being burned by carelessness, insincerity, or simple selfishness, we convince ourselves that the only way we are going to make it is if we do it alone. We focus on taking care of ourselves, without depending on others who may disappoint us again.

But the truth remains—we are not an island unto ourselves. We affect others. We need others. We regularly either encourage or discourage others by the content and tone of our interaction with them, or the lack of it. If we try to survive on our own, we will eventually fail, especially when the floodwaters come. We were never supposed to be able to do it all alone. The creation of humanity started with the formation of a couple because they were destined to help each other, as are we to this day. Finding your own way by your own strength is a foreign concept in the mind of God.

The New Testament contains at least twenty distinct commands for believers that specifically involve the phrase "one another." The list is all-encompassing: love one another (John 13:34), be devoted to one another (Romans 12:10), live in harmony with one another (Romans 12:16), don't judge one another (Romans 14:13), accept one another (Romans 15:7), instruct one another (Romans 15:14), greet one another with a holy kiss (Romans 16:16), serve one another (Galatians 5:13), bear with one another (Ephesians 4:2), be kind and compassionate to one another (Ephesians 4:32), submit to one another (Ephesians 5:21), forgive one another (Colossians 3:13), admonish one another (Colossians 3:16), encourage one another (1 Thessalonians 5:11), spur one another on toward good deeds (Hebrews 10:24), offer hospitality to one another (1 Peter 4:9), and the list goes on. The Christian life does not have a solo option.

Going it alone is a human concept, propagated particularly for men by the media. Whether it be Seagal, Van Damme, the Lone Ranger, or Schwarzenegger, the movie tough guy always defeats the bad guys single-handedly. But as I said, this is human thinking, and so, it is wrong.

Being totally responsible for yourself can feel like the noble and courageous thing to do, but to think like God sees human interaction in a different light. Yes, we need to be responsible, self-starting people who are not a total drain on everyone around us. The Apostle Paul referred to this as *"each man . . . bearing his own load"* (Galatians 6:5 NASB). But in the same passage, he also says, *"Bear one another's burdens, and thus fulfill the law of Christ"* (Galatians 6:2 NASB).

Within this brief passage we have God's perspective on human relations in a nutshell. Don't be a slouch. Carry your own weight. Don't take advantage of Christian charity by making a nuisance of yourself. But when it comes time to deal with heavy burdens, we should help bear those for each other. God never intended for us to struggle with the tough stuff all alone.

And he didn't create us to be an entity by ourselves. Paul reminds the believers in the city of Corinth, *"Don't you realize that your bodies are actually parts of Christ?"* (1 Corinthians 6:15). God-like thinking grasps the profound truth of the indwelling Christ. How can we continue to see ourselves as individual separate units when we are actually one of many members formed together into the body of Christ, the church?

According to 1 Corinthians 12, though we may be diverse, we all fit uniquely together into one functioning body that operates successfully as a whole (12:18–20). Though some members of the body may look more prominent than others, all parts are needed (12:21–24) and every member is to be cared for (12:25). As well, suffering and rejoicing with each other should be a natural part of the way we interact (12:26).

Functioning together properly as a healthy body also involves regularly gathering together for fellowship and encouragement (Hebrews 10:25). There is a growing tendency today for disgruntled or disillusioned twenty-first century believers to avoid church gatherings, choosing instead to stay home and watch a great speaker on a favorite Sunday morning television program. As real as the church-hurt may be, and as good as the weekly sermon may seem, we are not doing it right when we forsake the assembling of ourselves together on a regular basis, whether it be in a home church or in a more traditional institutionalized setting. God never intended for us to do it alone. We must make an attempt to find some place to fellowship with other members of the body.

The support and encouragement of other believers is needed, particularly because of the spiritual warfare that surrounds us as serious followers. Satan hates us and wants to destroy us, especially if we show any spiritual interest at all. If we are engaged in developing our relationship with God, the devil and his demons will go after us to bring us down until we are so discouraged that we want to throw in the towel on Christianity.

At this very moment, there is a battle for our souls going on in the spiritual realm. We can't see the battle. Sometimes we may not even feel it, though many times we do—it feels like discouragement and disillusionment with God. When we feel ourselves losing our faith and our desire to obey God or be close to him, we are being assaulted spiritually.

The angels of God are fighting for us, but we must fight too. We must make a concerted effort to resist the devil. We fight him by praying; we fight by turning to the Word of God; we fight by holding on to what we know to be true; we fight by surrounding our minds with every aspect of God's salvation; we fight by making our feet take us away from places that will dishonor the gospel and cause us to fall (Ephesians 6:14–17).

But we were not meant to fight alone. Spiritual battles are best won when we fight them together with other people of faith. Many times we cannot struggle through successfully alone; we need to band together in order to be victorious, just like I needed the help of my wife and daughter to be victorious over the rising water in my window wells.

You see, the struggles that we face when we take God seriously are much like rising flood water. Flood water swells rapidly, and once it gets to a certain level, there is not much we can do to repel it, especially if we are by ourselves. When we determine to walk with Jesus, the challenges we face are huge. Fleshly lusts, envious desires, and arrogant attitudes may assault us from the outside or may rise up furiously from the inside.

It is impossible to fully understand the power of sin until we deliberately try to resist it. As C. S. Lewis says,

Only those who try to resist temptation know how strong it is ... A man who gives into temptation after five minutes simply does not know what it would have been like an hour later. That is why bad people, in one sense, know very little about badness. They have lived a sheltered life by always giving in. We never find out the strength of the evil impulse inside us until we try to fight it.[7]

And this battle cannot be won without help.

We need each other! We need assistance in the spiritual battles that we face. It is so very difficult, if not impossible, to walk the Christian life alone. Even the godly King Joash, who followed the Lord closely for many years, collapsed spiritually when his mentor and helper, the chief priest, Jehoiada, died. 2 Chronicles 24:17–18 says,

> But after Jehoiada's death, the leaders of Judah came and bowed before King Joash and persuaded him to listen to their advice. They decided to abandon the Temple of the Lord, the God of their ancestors, and they worshiped Asherah poles and idols instead! Because of this sin, divine anger fell on Judah and Jerusalem.

The Apostle Paul, perhaps the greatest follower of Christ of all time, knew the importance of surrounding himself with good people. In almost every letter that he writes to the churches he planted, he acknowledges the people who helped him. He admits times of discouragement and spiritual attack, but he always had people around him to assist him in the struggle.

There is probably no better illustration of this than the lengthy final remarks in Paul's letter to the church in the city of Rome. In the first sixteen verses of the last chapter, Paul sends affectionate greetings to at least 30 different people who encouraged or supported him in his ministry. The letter then closes with a list of seven other individuals besides Paul who were working with him in his ministry at that time. Paul valued people and always had a gaggle of them around him to assist him in the battle and to keep him from being overwhelmed. Do we have a list of people in our lives who are dedicated to helping us become successful Christians?

---

[7] C. S. Lewis, *Mere Christianity* as viewed online at http://usminc.org/
FLASHGIFS/MereChristianitybyCSLewis.pdf (accessed Nov. 21, 2008).

Who can help us fight back the flood of worldliness and strengthen us in our battle against temptation? If there is no one on our list, we need to remedy that. We need to have a plan to surround ourselves with people to assist us in our spiritual walk. We need someone to push us on and challenge us when we make poor decisions. Maybe it's a grandparent we can connect with. Maybe there's an old acquaintance who we know is a committed Christian. Maybe we need to get ourselves connected with our old church. Maybe we need to find a new church. Maybe we need to text or email someone regularly who can be an accountability cyber-buddy for us.

Whatever it takes, do it. We must find people to help us so we can grow together. We were never meant to fly solo. On that fateful night in my basement, if I had been alone when the flood rains came, I would have been overwhelmed; I would have been defeated; I would have lost the battle.

If we want to walk with Jesus, we can't put ourselves in the position of trying to battle the flood of spiritual warfare alone. We must create a network around us so we can win, so we can defeat the devil's schemes against us and continue to walk strongly in the Lord. The Master is saying, "You need help; I never intended for you to do it alone."

Chapter 20

"Get used to disappointment."

*"But as I looked at everything I had worked
so hard to accomplish, it was all so meaningless—
like chasing the wind."*

~Ecclesiastes 2:1

Living in a fallen world guarantees us at least two things: plenty of surprises and plenty of disappointments. This world in itself sets us up for perpetual sadness and frustration. The attractions that lure us leave us feeling empty. The possessions we cherish break or wear out. The people we trust violate our goodwill. The dreams we chase never appease the angst we thought would be cured by their arrival. And, so often, the person we are is not the person we wish we were. From the confusion of young adulthood to the silly crises of midlife to the disenchantment of old age, we wrestle with the gaping chasm that exists between our expectations and our real life experience.

As a young man with every possible opportunity available to him, King Solomon expected to get some great mileage out of his vast wealth and ample leisure time. Certainly, the richest man alive would have the best chance of anyone to orchestrate his surroundings to create a fulfilling life. Hoping to feel a stupendous rush from his many economic, cultural, architectural, and sexual achievements, Solomon instead experienced a tremendous let down. All his hard work felt as useless as chasing wind. In his own words, there was *"no profit"* from any of his labors (Ecclesiastes 2:11 NASB). Such feelings of disillusionment should not surprise us, for there is nothing in this world that delivers what it promises. We are made by God and he alone can satisfy our thirsts. The world entices us to dig wells for other sources of water in alternate locations, but as Jeremiah says, these are but *"broken cisterns that can hold no water"* (Jeremiah 2:13 NASB).

The things of this world have a certain obscure and illusive essence to them, somewhat like the shadowy images in Plato's *Allegory of the Cave*. The worldly things with which we interact are mere shadows or copies of what is truly real, what truly matters.

We want to live happy and productive lives. We want to love and be loved. We get up each day and go to work or school or busy ourselves with household tasks, hoping to feel that our existence is meaningful. Even though we may experience our fair share of joyful delights as we go about our day, there is always a gnawing sensation of incompleteness, a feeling that something is missing. We experience this annoying emotion because something *is* missing: God.

Pure love exists, but only in God. Shadows of that love reside in us and in the ones who care about us, but only dimly. *"We know how much God loves us, and we have put our trust in his love. God is love, and all who live in love live in God, and God lives in them"* (1 John 4:16).

Pure light exists, but only in God. We may temporarily follow a counterfeit beacon with strong potential, but eventually that worldly light runs out or leads us into the dark. Jesus said, *"I am the light of the world. If you follow me, you won't have to walk in darkness, because you will have the light that leads to life"* (John 8:12).

Pure nourishment exists, but only in God. A good steak tastes great, but in five hours we are hungry again, and in twenty-four hours, it's totally behind us. Jesus said, *"I am the bread of life. Whoever comes to me will never be hungry again. Whoever believes in me will never be thirsty"* (John 6:35).

Pure safety and security exist, but only in God. In this world, we use every means possible to defend ourselves from harm, but to no avail. Thieves break in; evil people hurt us; good people hurt us. Though we are never fully safe in this world, we are safe in the arms of God. *"The eternal God is your refuge, and his everlasting arms are under you. He drives out the enemy before you"* (Deuteronomy 33:27).

Pure sustenance exists, but only in God. Jesus said, *"I am the vine; you are the branches. Those who remain in me, and I in them, will produce much fruit. For apart from me you can do nothing"* (John 15:5). Human thinking has trouble believing this, so we continue to flail away independently, amassing our own big pile of nothing.

Pure relational harmony exists, but only in God. The members of the trinity function in perfect synchronization and pristine fellowship. One day, Christ and his bride, the church, will be unified in an eternal state of ideal communion. Until then, we will fumble around and forge ahead in our attempts to create meaningful community, continually experiencing dissatisfaction with its paleness in comparison to the real thing.

These good and satisfying entities exist in their purest form, but only in God.

This fallen world provides but pale copies of the one true reality, which is God. At times, the copies seem to be good enough, all we need to live a happy life. We are elated with young married life but then we grow up. We are enamored with our young children but then they grow up. We achieve our goals only to find someone stole the treasure at the top of the mountain. Every ounce and ton of disappointment causes our souls to feel that twinge of eternity, and we know there must be more.

Besides the trickery of even decent earthly pleasures, our hearts groan at the volume of unfairness we may be forced to swallow on our life's journey. Every pundit sage worth his or her salt has a "life's not fair" adage included in their arsenal. According to a human comprehension of justice and equality, rarely do the proper people receive the proper treatment for their proper behavior.

Good things happen to bad people and bad things happen to good people. Careless doctors misdiagnose and the cancer is not spotted soon enough. Lazy teachers fail to enhance the learning opportunities of children and cause them to miss out on their full potential. Reckless drivers take one too many chances and snuff out the life of a precious daughter in her youth. Indeed, from many angles, it appears that life in this world is not fair.

But this world does something even worse to the wayward soul than just fooling us with pale copies of the one true reality or dealing us the occasional unfair hand. This world system, influenced and orchestrated by the devil, the *"god of this age"* (2 Corinthians 4:4 NIV), produces a smoke and mirrors circus show of monstrous proportions that tricks its travelers into lustful and destructive allurements. There is untold heartache for the fool who is overwhelmed by worldliness. Oh, the disappointment of sin! *"For everything in the world—the cravings of sinful man, the lust of the eyes, and the boasting of what he or she does—comes not from the Father but from the world"* (1 John 2:16 NIV).

So, we are disappointed by good things because they leave us feeling empty; we are disappointed by unfair situations because we crave immediate justice; and we are disappointed by sin because its pleasures quickly pass. Everything apart from God will lead us to some form of dissatisfaction. Whether it be a nice dinner in a fancy restaurant or a disastrous drinking binge to solve some personal problem, human actions that do not involve the Creator in some form birth disillusionment. For all of us living in a fallen world, God's advice is plain—get used to disappointment.

But I must say that it's okay for it to be that way. Disappointment is okay. In fact, it is a good thing. Frustration with life can be very useful for our eternal state. Brokenness can be a very solid foundation for the construction of a new and better life. Disappointment reminds us of what is real. It drives us back to God. God is constantly giving us what we need. And what we need sometimes is more disappointment to stop us from getting too comfortable, too settled in the world. Otherwise, we get confused, thinking this world is all there is, thinking this world's experiences, in and of themselves, comprise all that there is to our existence.

No, we were created for more than merely positive experiences of good meals, nice homes, happy family times, and exciting sporting events. There is more. There is the kingdom of God and a heavenly future mysteriously tied to our performance during the rehearsal down here on earth.

The Scriptures exhort us to adopt a proper understanding of our human lives on this third rock from the sun. This world is supposed to feel foreign to us. Paul reminds us that *"our citizenship is in heaven, from which also we eagerly wait for the Savior, the Lord Jesus Christ"* (Philippians 3:20 NASB). Peter says it this way: *"Dear friends, I urge you, as aliens and strangers in the world, to abstain from sinful desires, which war against your soul"* (1 Peter 2:11 NIV). And when Jesus prayed to his Father just before he was betrayed by Judas, he said, referring to his followers, *"They do not belong to this world any more than I do"* (John 17:16). This world is supposed to feel foreign and uncomfortable because it has been tainted by sin.

Thinking like God involves perceiving life in this fallen world as more of a journey than a destination. When we consider our earthly life to be the destination, we become focused on the concept of arrival. This is the root cause of the disappointment in our lives. We work hard to arrive (new job, new home, new car, new wife), and the arrival leaves us a bit flat. If we saw our earthly lives properly, as a journey home to heaven, we might be able to focus more clearly on our true destination.

Vacations are fun but they can also be a bit annoying at times. Soaring gas prices trouble our minds and our pocketbooks, restaurant food grows old quickly, and sometimes motel beds leave our backs reeling in agony. We have fun, and it's nice to get away, but there is something wonderfully settling about the thought of coming home.

That we are offered an eternal future, an eternal home, with our heavenly Father is a spectacular gift, largely unrecognized by the majority of humans and amazingly underappreciated by Christians themselves. A heavenly home is most cherished and anticipated by those who have experienced the most earthly disappointment. Those deprived of sufficient suffering hold little regard for the prize of heaven.

The Apostle Paul had more than his fair share of disappointment and discouraging life experiences. He writes,

> Yet what we suffer now is nothing compared to the glory he will reveal to us later. For all creation is waiting eagerly for that future day when God will reveal who his children really are. Against its will, all creation was subjected to God's curse. But with eager hope, the creation looks forward to the day when it will join God's children in glorious freedom from death and decay. For we know that all creation has been groaning as in the pains of childbirth right up to the present time. And we believers also groan, even though we have the Holy Spirit within us as a foretaste of future glory, for we long for our bodies to be released from sin and suffering. We, too, wait with eager hope for the day when God will give us our full rights as his adopted children, including the new bodies he has promised us. We were given this hope when we were saved. (Romans 8:18–24)

Paul understood what Jesus was talking about when he said, *"Here on earth you will have many trials and sorrows."* But Paul also understood the rest of that verse: *"But take heart, because I have overcome the world"* (John 16:33). Amidst the tribulation of this fallen world, we can have peace in our hearts because we know that the disappointment is not final; it is only part of the story, and the story has a happy ending for the people of faith.

When we live selfishly, we are certain to be severely disappointed. Doing what comes naturally and living self-centeredly leads to colossal disillusionment, emptiness, and futility. Human self-absorption may be addictive, but the obsession brings nothing but a famine to the satisfaction of our souls. Selfish people are rarely content. At the end of the day, doing something for someone else usually feels better than doing something for ourselves. Even atheistic philanthropists experience emotional pleasure when they care for the needs of others as well as their own.

But life is not just about doing good deeds, though they are necessary (Titus 2:14); it is about doing the will of our heavenly Father in the midst of disappointment. And when we do his will, we have a better chance of keeping our focus on heaven and a better chance of not being overwhelmed by distress. But do not be fooled—even when we try to live right for God, we will be disappointed at times.

We will be disappointed by things, by people, by ourselves. We may even be disappointed by God. We are disappointed by people because they are no better than we are. Usually, we are disappointed by God because we make him out to be someone he is not. Erroneously, we fancy him to be a genie in a bottle and then blame him for failing to deliver us our wishes.

Of course, one of the most tragic consequences of human thinking regarding earthly disappointment is the temptation to slide into a quagmire of bitterness in response to the trials and sadness that envelop our souls.

Bitterness comes from bad thinking.

Failing to see the value of earthly disappointment leads us to search for a cure, a quick fix that will make everything better, that will allow us to feel good again. When the panacea does not arrive in time, we become bitter. We convince ourselves that we do not deserve the heartbreak. We tell ourselves that we have behaved well enough to merit something better than the trial tossed our way. We grow irritated, even angry. Then we sin some more, bringing upon ourselves even more disappointment.

This state of bitterness is one of the most horrid conditions of a fallen humanity. We must make every effort to avoid this pitfall of human thinking. We must remind each other, and ourselves, that, through the fall of mankind and the ensuing curse, God has deliberately allowed the temporal world to work the way it does. It is programmed to fail. It is programmed to disappoint.

And it has been set up that way to push us back to God. Ironically, as we chase material pleasures and solutions to our problems, God uses disappointment to make our hungry hearts hungry for him. The frustration is supposed to feel frustrating. But instead of becoming bitter, we need to become better. We need to trust God and surrender our tattered hearts in complete abandonment to the one who knows every corner of our being.

The facts are clear—we just need to straighten out our thinking and draw closer to the mind of God. It is no surprise. We will be disappointed. Get used to it. Let that disappointment do its good work in our lives. But instead of allowing the fog of bitterness to roll over our souls, we need to let it drive us back to God, where we belong.

Instead of bleating for deliverance like pathetic sheep in distress, pray for strength to make it through with the dignity and courage that our Savior clothed himself with on his journey to the cross. And like Christ heading to the cross, this act of ultimate disappointment in the eyes of his close followers was but part of a journey to a most glorious future.

Chapter 21

"I love a good paradox."

"Those who love their life in this world will lose it.
Those who care nothing for their life in this world
will keep it for eternal life."

~John 12:25

Paradoxes perplex us. They leave us feeling like we don't know the final answer to the question, and that bothers us. We like to understand everything clearly and have all our ideas and explanations fit into neat little boxes. We don't enjoy apparent contradictions because we cannot believe that opposites can coexist or that the right answer is something contrary to what rational western thinking would conclude. Though it may never fully make sense to us this side of eternity, to think like God involves reveling in the mysteries of a good paradox.

Where do we begin? The Scriptures are laden with these mysteries. How can a good God allow evil to permeate his creation? How does Moses see God without dying? How is it possible for God to change his mind about something?

Perhaps we should start with the birth of Christ, one of the greatest paradoxes of all. How can we ever understand the incarnation? Jesus originated within Mary's womb, contrary to the laws of life. And then for the next nine months, the second person of the trinity was subject to the diet and habits of an obscure teenage girl, unmarried at that.

As the Savior arrived on the scene, several more paradoxes became apparent. First, how could this little baby in the manger be both fully man and fully God? How can 100% + 100% = 1? Our natural minds cannot grasp the concept of the two coexisting in the same person. It is baffling to think that the Creator of the universe could be limited to the flesh of a squirming infant.

What a paradox to see the King of Kings with his newborn life in danger! The vulnerability of the Christ child as recorded in the second chapter of Matthew is an arcane mystery. Unlike a typical earthly king, God in the flesh put himself at our mercy, where we could do him harm, even kill him. The angry and hateful actions of a jealous human King Herod sent the Messiah King running into hiding in Egypt until the murderer himself died. Even then, Joseph was forced to take his wife and little boy far away from Judea because Herod's successor also posed a threat to the safety of Jesus.

From the very start—as a baby and then as a small child whisked away into hiding—Jesus' task was not one that would be done from strength, but rather, vulnerability, exposure, and eventually death. God the Father mysteriously crafted it that way. This is not how a human would script the revelation of a Savior for the world. We would make him stronger and less susceptible to harm—but God made him weak.

This weak strength of the Savior characterized much of his life on earth. He was raised as the son of a simple carpenter in a spit of a town with a history of producing nobodies. When he was twelve years old, he confounded the most brilliant Jewish scholars on the planet but on the same day was scolded by his parents for not staying with the group during their trip home from Jerusalem. When he started to gain notoriety as an adult, his siblings and hometown acquaintances couldn't understand what the fuss was all about.

Jesus spent 33 years on this planet in human skin but did nothing publicly for the first 30 of them. Though he himself formed this earth's majestic mountain ranges and vast oceans by the word of his mouth, he traveled no further than 70 miles from his birthplace during his adult life. Throughout his ministry, Jesus had nowhere to lay his head. The Maker of many heavenly mansions had not even a small home to call his own. Basically, he was a kept man, taken care of by women.

When it came time to pick his roster for a supporting ministry cast, the omniscient Son of God picked unlearned, cowardly social outcasts, including a criminal and a thief. Much to the amazement of onlookers, the spotless Lamb of God partied with sinners and lambasted religious leaders. He delivered a crazed man who was possessed by thousands of demons and helped a hooker escape being stoned, restoring her dignity in the process. He gave sinners second chances but wrote off religious hypocrites. How could this be God in the flesh? He looked and sounded too unreligious.

When he demonstrated his power, he showed us that he could heal any disease, exorcise any demon, and tame the raging winds of a storm with but an effortless utterance from his lips; and yet, the omnipotent Son of God was unable to make a sullen human heart soft against its will.

That he could control the time of his execution tells us that he had the power to escape or to surrender his body over to his enemies at his own discretion. He said to his disciples, *"No one can take my life from me. I sacrifice it voluntarily. For I have the authority to lay it down when I want to and also to take it up again"* (John 10:18). If Jesus controlled the time of his crucifixion, why did he cut his earthly ministry so short when so many others could have been helped and healed by its augmentation?

When he spoke, he often used parables so the general population would not understand what he was talking about. To his followers he said, *"To you it has been granted to know the mysteries of the kingdom of God, but to the rest it is in parables, so that seeing they may not see, and hearing they may not understand"* (Luke 8:10 NASB).

The teachings of Jesus are full of paradoxes that defy natural human comprehension. He spoke of losing one's life to save it (Mark 8:35). He said those who assume the bottom positions and serve everyone will end up in first place (Mark 9:35). Some people who cling to first place now will end up in last place (Luke 13:30). He said the one who exalts himself will be humbled and the one who humbles himself will be exalted (Luke 18:14). He said only children can enter his kingdom (Luke 18:17). And he also said the way to create unfailing treasure is to sell all your possessions and give them to charity (Luke 12:33). Saving by losing, securing first place by being last, humbled to be exalted, a kingdom of children, treasures amassed by giving everything away—these concepts do not gel with normal human thought. But neither do most of the things Jesus said.

Jesus exhorted us to invite only poor people to our parties so there is no chance of them repaying us (Luke 14:13–14). He said if we truly want to follow him, we must hate the members of our families (Luke 14:26). Instead of peace, he said he came for the purpose of causing division on the earth (Luke 12:49–53, Matthew 10:34). He said even if we accumulate an abundance of possessions, we have not altered the true state of our lives (Luke 12:15). And when he prayed to his Father, he thanked him for revealing his spiritual truths to the simple people in the world rather than the wise (Luke 10:21).

Not only do these teachings go against our natural grain, some of them seem to contradict other passages in the Scriptures. After all, are not husbands supposed to love their wives, and fathers, their children? Did not the angels at Christ's birth say something about his arrival being connected to peace on earth? Wouldn't it be more productive to reveal spiritual truth to wise people with their network of connections who could pass it on more efficiently and effectively than the poor and the weak?

The words of Jesus can be very confusing at times. When a potential disciple asked him for a chance to bury his dead father before proceeding on with the Savior, Jesus said, *"Follow me and allow the dead to bury their own dead"* (Matthew 8:22 NASB). When he sent his disciples out on a missions trip, he exhorted them to be *"shrewd as serpents and innocent as doves"* (Matthew 10:16 NASB). And when he taught his followers about revenge, it involved offering the assailant another body part he has not yet hit as well as giving the thief another article of your clothes that he failed to steal the first time (Luke 6:29).

For another catalog of paradoxes, check out the Sermon on the Mount in Matthew 5. The poor in spirit are promised a kingdom. Those who are mourning are promised comforting. The meek get the earth in the end. Only righteous appetites get satisfied. And the proper response to persecution and reviling should be happiness and joy.

Right up until his death, there are incomprehensible mysteries continually emerging in the story. Speaking of his impending death, Jesus said these words to his friends: *"Unless a kernel of wheat is planted in the soil and dies, it remains alone. But its death will produce many new kernels— a plentiful harvest of new lives"* (John 12:24). It is hard for us to fathom a good side to death.

Even the logistics of the last hours of Christ's life are puzzling. Just before Gethsemane, Jesus told his disciples to make sure they had a sword (Luke 22:36). He even encouraged them to sell something if necessary in order to purchase the weapon. But then, in the garden, Peter was scolded for using his sword in defense of the Master. Even on the cross there are inexplicable things happening—human nerve endings suffering extreme torturous sensations are the basis for a divine and miraculous work of propitiation being recorded in heaven. I don't get it.

And what about the whole notion of atonement? Blood cleansing? How can that be?

And it doesn't get any easier when we read the rest of the New Testament. Many of Jesus' paradoxical themes are woven into the fabric of the epistles. Paul speaks of foolishness and wisdom.

Remember, dear brothers and sisters, that few of you were wise in the world's eyes or powerful or wealthy when God called you. Instead, God chose things the world considers foolish in order to shame those who think they are wise. And he chose things that are powerless to shame those who are powerful. God chose things despised by the world, things counted as nothing at all, and used them to bring to nothing what the world considers important. (1 Corinthians 1:26-28)

And again,

Stop deceiving yourselves. If you think you are wise by this world's standards, you need to become a fool to be truly wise. (1 Corinthians 3:18)

In several of his epistles, Paul also spoke of the importance of rejoicing in persecution. Writing to the church at Philippi, he says, *"For to you it has been granted for Christ's sake, not only to believe in him, but also to suffer for his sake"* (Philippians 1:29 NASB). Suffering for Christ is a gift that has been granted from God, even a "calling," as the Apostle Peter describes it (1 Peter 2:21 NASB).

Regarding the paradox of strength in weakness and his own struggle with asking God to remove the thorn in the flesh from his life, Paul writes,

Each time he (Jesus) said, "My grace is all you need. My power works best in weakness." So now I am glad to boast about my weaknesses, so that the power of Christ can work through me. That's why I take pleasure in my weaknesses, and in the insults, hardships, persecutions, and troubles that I suffer for Christ. For when I am weak, then I am strong. (2 Corinthians 12:9–10)

Strength through weakness. Joy from suffering. Give to get. Die to live. Broken to be beautiful. Power in surrender. The list of paradoxes goes on and on.

Why is God's Word laced with such a litany of apparent contradictions and paradoxes? Why isn't the Bible more simple and straightforward?

Perhaps God has designed it this way to remind us that he is God and we are not. As much as a pet cannot comprehend the actions of its master, we cannot humanly comprehend the full behavior of God.

So how do we handle this? Certainly, some of the Bible's apparent contradictions and paradoxes can be resolved easily, but others cannot. What do we do with the tough ones? Perhaps God wants us to spend less time figuring things out and more time just accepting things for what they are. Perhaps he wants us to simply trust him more. A great deal of rest can come to our souls when we learn to acknowledge paradoxes for what they are and appreciate our inability to reconcile them. Our best logic is still human logic and may not be God's logic.

For example, consider the discussion surrounding the sovereignty of God and the free will of man. One possible reconciliation of this great paradox is to say that these apparent contradictory notions are, in reality, two rails of a railway track, running side by side forever into glory without ever touching. Both are true, but operate independently and cooperatively in a mysterious fashion. Now, as quaint as that explanation may seem, like most other attempts to clarify the mysterious, it has the sense of skirting around the problem rather than explaining it satisfactorily.

We want to control ideas. We want to be able to wrap our minds around these mystifying thoughts. Human thinking naturally operates this way. We like to figure things out because then we have a sense of being done, completed— something else can now be checked off our list and done with. We don't like open-ended, confusing situations, but they are a big part of our reality as people of faith. And if we treat our lives as a journey, a pilgrimage, we may be less hung up on trying to get everything categorized and able to enjoy the ride a little more.

We must face the facts: some things cannot be resolved by any volume of human thought or verbiage. Biblical paradoxes of divine origin must, instead, be embraced—even reveled in. Focus on what you can learn about yourself rather than what you think you should know about the big picture. Use these paradoxes as an opportunity to marvel at the greatness and glory of our holy God. Use them as an occasion to remind yourself of your smallness. Use them as a prompt to love more and boast less. Let them instruct you in humility and vulnerability.

As I said earlier, the Savior came to this earth in a paradoxical framework of vulnerability. And mysteriously, even today, God puts himself at risk as he entrusts himself to frail humans who flail away in their humanity, seeking to follow the Savior. Jesus is still vulnerable to assaults and criticisms as he resides in our hearts and is held responsible for our mistakes and our hypocrisies. Why does God continue to put himself at risk and make himself vulnerable by entrusting his reputation to humans? It is another one of his many mysteries; it is the way God does it and so it is right.

We must give up this compulsion to impose order and human logic on every situation or loss. We would do better to imagine our time on earth as a journey through a wilderness with some friends; you are not responsible to find a way out. You don't have to be an expert; just curiously meander in the maze and hold on to God. Embrace the ambiguity of life with your heart; don't over-analyze it with your head. If you are going to learn to think like God, learn to revel in the mysteries of a good paradox.

Chapter 22

"Trust me."

"Instead of trusting in our own strength or wits to get out of it, we were forced to trust God totally—not a bad idea since he's the God who raises the dead."

~2 Corinthians 1:9 MSG

In the grand scheme of human history, many civilizations have come and gone. Great cultures have risen and then fallen. Empires have grown to a place of dominance and then, over time, have all but disappeared. Think of all the ancient civilizations that once held a place of prominence but are now just a memory, or at best, a tourist attraction: Egypt, Persia, Babylon, Harappa, Maya, Greece, and Rome. These and many other civilizations emerged and dutifully dissipated, leaving behind a legacy as well as some ruins: Egyptian pyramids; Greek arts and philosophy; Roman roads, government, and law; a Phoenician alphabet; a Chinese wall; and a story of a general crossing the Alps with a herd of war elephants.

History is fascinating because it explores the great mysteries of past human civilizations. But the bottom line for empires and powerful civilizations is that they have a finite lifespan. Bits and pieces are passed on to future generations, but the basic form and power structure of the civilization eventually collapses.

Why am I saying this? What is the point of this little history lesson? Human thinking can be very forgetful and dense. We westerners living in Europe and North America need to be reminded that we are no different than the civilizations of the past. Like great empires of foregone days, we ourselves are part of a civilization that has risen and will one day fall.

We belong to what is referred to as modern western civilization. Our civilization began to rise in seventeenth-century Europe when absolute monarchs like Louis XIV brought stability to a continent ravaged by years of political and religious warfare. Their support of scientific advancement, the arts, and world exploration allowed for the development of a powerful civilization that has come to dominate world affairs for the past 400 years.

Over these years, modern western civilization has come to treasure certain ideals as being critical to her continuing strength, things such as industrialization, mass media, capitalism, civil rights, democracy, and technological advancement, especially in the area of the military.

The leader of western civilization since the end of World War I until now has been, of course, the United States. America has done a pretty good job of running a world empire. As a Canadian, my nation has enjoyed the peace and security of living next door to the friendly emperor. And for a long time now, it has seemed that western civilization is invincible, leading us to believe that it will exist indefinitely.

9-11 showed us differently. That day reminded us that powerful empires *are* vulnerable! They are vulnerable to time, they are vulnerable to internal decay and apathy, and they are vulnerable to people who don't play by the rules. Regardless of who was behind the events of that day, it proved that earthly security is never a given. Just as the fourth- and fifth-century barbarians began to pick away at the Roman Empire on the frontiers, the enemies of the west have begun their assault on our culture, our way of life, and our position of world superiority.

So, in light of the fact that all great civilizations eventually fall, my question is this: What are we trusting in today? A godly king once said, *"Put your trust in the LORD your God and you will be established"* (2 Chronicles 20:20 NASB). Are we trusting in God or are we actually trusting in modern western civilization to somehow save the day? Allow me to elaborate.

I am convinced that many Christians have inadvertently come to mistake modern western civilization for the kingdom of God. Let me repeat that. I think that many believers have unknowingly mistaken our civilization in the west for the kingdom of God because of our Christian heritage, our rich history of missionary work to foreign lands, and the long and powerful duration of our existence.

Because we consider ourselves to be the closest thing to a godly society on this planet, we are in danger of convincing ourselves that our civilization is the beginning phase of God's rule on this earth. Most probably, this is an ill-conceived notion. Don't misunderstand me; I believe God blesses societies and nations that honor him and his principles of holiness, but if we try to equate the kingdom of God with modern western civilization, are we forgetting about our myopic self-centeredness, our materialism, our hedonism, and Hollywood?

No, our civilization is not the kingdom of God on earth. The kingdom of God is coming to earth, but modern western civilization as a whole will not likely be its main participant. The Day of the Lord is approaching, when Jesus Christ returns to save the righteous and punish the wicked on earth and firmly establish his kingdom forever. To truly be ready for that day, we need to be trusting in God and not in our civilization.

So what does it mean to trust in a civilization as opposed to trusting in God? As thirsty humans, we long for peace and security so we can live prosperously, significantly, and productively. The ancient Chinese trusted in a wall for their security against the invading Mongols. The aristocrats of ancient Rome trusted in their army to secure them from rebellious tribes on the fringes of their empire. The prosperous ancient empires of Central America trusted in their isolation and their pagan gods for their future security until the Spanish arrived with horses, guns, and small pox.

I wonder if we are doing the same thing today. Are we propping up our lives on shaky pillars? I can think of at least four sources of false hope within western civilization that could attract our trust, especially in these days of uncertainty. These could be identified as our military, our economy, our leaders, and our playful distractions.

Instead of trusting in God, some of us might be trusting in the military might of the west. Perhaps we believe that America's incredible military strength will bring about an eventual victory over her terrorist enemies so everything can go back to being "normal" again. If this is our source of hope and security, we need to study the history of the Vietnam Conflict and we need to re-read our Bibles. Let's not talk about Vietnam, but what do the Scriptures say about trusting in military might?

In ancient history, the equivalent to military strength was the possession of many horses. Owning a large cavalry became the symbol of great national power. Because God wanted his chosen people to trust in him alone, he forbade the Israelites from amassing large numbers of horses. Eventually, they disobeyed him in this area and things did not go well for them.

Listen to the scriptural warnings about trusting in military prowess more than God: *"Don't count on your warhorse to give you victory—for all its strength, it cannot save you"* (Psalm 33:17). Isaiah wrote, *"Woe to those who . . . rely on horses, and trust in chariots because they are many, and in horsemen because they are very strong, but they do not . . .*

seek the Lord" (Isaiah 31:1 NASB). Perhaps no passage addresses this issue more clearly than Psalm 147:10–11. "*He takes no pleasure in the strength of a horse or in human might. No, the Lord's delight is in those who fear him, those who put their hope in his unfailing love.*" Beware of trusting in the mesmerizing military power of the west. No miracle weapons under construction now or in the future will ever be able to provide us with absolute peace and security. To think like God means to trust him alone.

Instead of trusting in God, some of us in the west might be holding to a false hope of economic security. If the stock market can just hang in there long enough and stave off another collapse, then we can all feel good about our investments and retirement plans.

Maybe for you it's not the markets but a family business. Perhaps you're feeling secure because you are poised to inherit a lucrative family business or a large family inheritance so you won't have to worry about financial security—or will you? How secure is our western economy? How secure is the whole monetary system? Germany 1923 is not that far from our memories. Are we trusting in the shakiness of monetary currency or are we trusting in God?

Remember the parable in Luke 12 of the rich fool who thought he was set for life because of a huge bumper crop. What was God's response to the man who thought he had a secure plan for his financial future? Luke 12:20 records the scathing words of God against him: "*You fool! This very night your soul is required of you; and now who will own what you have prepared?*" (NASB) God said, "It's time to meet me face to face. What good are all your barns? What have you been trusting in?"

God's thinking is very clear on this matter: "*Instruct those who are rich in this present world not to be conceited or to fix their hope on the uncertainty of riches, but on God, who richly supplies us with all things to enjoy*" (1 Timothy 6:17 NASB). Beware of trusting in our western myth of economic security.

Instead of trusting in God, some people in the west find themselves trusting in human leadership. Historically, some of our leaders have been decent and reasonable. Others have been quite arrogant about their abilities. Have we fooled ourselves into thinking that our problems can be solved and world tensions resolved by strong human leadership—by men and women who will use their education, their incredible reasoning powers, and their eloquent oratory abilities to devise and execute clever solutions to tough problems? What does God say about human wisdom?

> *Let no man deceive himself. If any man among you thinks he is wise in this age, let him become foolish that he may become wise. For the wisdom of this world is foolishness before God. For it is written, "He is the one who catches the wise in their craftiness"; and again, "The Lord knows the reasonings of the wise that they are useless." So then let no one boast in men.* (1 Corinthians 3:18–21 NASB)

The Psalmist adds,

> *It is better to take refuge in the Lord than to trust in man. It is better to take refuge in the Lord than to trust in princes.* (Psalm 118:8–9 NASB)

So God instructs us to avoid trusting in our military might, our economic plans, and the wisdom of men. What else is there besides God? Unfortunately, modern western civilization offers a lot of personal comforts and physical distractions that can detract us from trusting God. A persecuted believer in China or the Sudan has no other option but to trust God. But in the west, when the world situation gets shaky or our personal lives start to crumble, we can simply resort to another diversion: the latest cool movie, an evening out with our friends, a new toy, or a good meal.

Perhaps we aren't even aware of it, but very often when our thirsty hearts long for security, we run to pleasurable activities to distract us from the fact that we are not trusting in

God for every aspect of our lives. The Apostle Paul warns about the outcome for people who walk according to their own physical desires as opposed to Christ:

> *For many walk, of whom I often told you, and now tell you even weeping, that they are enemies of the cross of Christ, whose end is destruction, whose god is their appetite (belly), and whose glory is in their shame, who set their minds on earthly things.* (Philippians 3:18–19 NASB)

Again I ask: What are we trusting in today? Like the many civilizations that have gone before us, modern western civilization has risen and, given enough time, will one day fall. We've already seen the cracks opening up. There will continue to be much denial about this fact, but our culture will certainly come to its demise one day.

Political leaders at every level will keep on assuring us that our way of life is intact because of our intelligence and our resolve. But they are wrong. One day, the Lord will bring true justice to this earth and every false source of strength will be exposed for what it is. When Jesus returns and everything about us is laid bare, what will be exposed as the source of our hope, as the root of our trust? Will it be some aspect of our civilization, our personal determination, or will it be God?

We need to ask the Lord to search our hearts and reveal to us any wicked way within us, any remnants of trust and hope that are being offered foolishly to things that won't come through for us, sources that won't deliver. Only God will be forever true to us, our temporal needs, and our eternal security. He alone is worthy and deserving of our trust.

Everything that I have said so far is the textbook answer. Allow me to get a little more personal as I reflect on why I should trust God.

I would have to say that I have had a pretty good life. Fortunately, I have known neither poverty nor persistent hunger. My parents loved me dearly and I enjoyed a healthy upbringing in many ways. But despite my basic good fortune,

I've had my share of pain and disappointments. I've experienced loneliness and sadness. I've gone through periods of my life where I've felt lost, depressed, and very sinful. Sometimes I've felt so distant from God, I thought he might never speak to me or hear me again. I don't fully understand the emotional swings of the fallen human condition. I don't know why I can slip away from God so quickly when it was just yesterday that I felt so close.

But in spite of how I may feel on any given day, there is one thing that I have come to know for sure, and that is this: God is taking care of me. Such a phrase does not mean that all will go smoothly. Sometimes I suffer because I need to be disciplined by the hand of God as his child. Sometimes I suffer for just being plain stupid in my decisions. Sometimes I suffer simply because I am living in a fallen world. But in the midst of all this—the hard times as well as all the many good times—I know in my heart that the God of the universe knows me intimately, loves me unconditionally, and is taking care of me. Often he is ordering my steps even when I am not aware of it.

As a child I never considered myself to be a klutz, but I had a lot of near-death mishaps. At eight, I fell on a vicious broken jar that sliced open my stomach. At ten, I carelessly biked into the path of an oncoming car and had to hit the ground to avoid being pummeled. At thirteen, I was creamed by a pick-up truck when my brother and I were coming home from Boys' Brigade. At fourteen, I chopped open my leg with an axe during a high school camping trip out in the middle of nowhere. At fifteen, I narrowly missed being sucked into a whirlpool at the bottom of some rapids when I was swimming in dangerous waters in a river in northern Ontario. And the list could go on. Especially in my youth, but also through my mature years, God has had his angels watching over me and has taken care of me.

As an adult with a few miles behind me, it's easy for me to see how the Lord's hand has been on my life—guiding me in certain directions, stopping me from doing things that would have been wasteful or destructive, exposing me to situations and challenges that have prepared me for tasks I did not anticipate.

God has not only guided my life through the routine and common affairs of day to day, he has also brought miracles my way so that I could see his love and power. I witnessed my best friend in high school give his heart to Jesus and then watched God deliver him from a lifestyle of horrid sin that he hated. I got to see a young female student of mine saved from a past plagued with sexual abuse and torture. God was even gracious enough to grant me a small physical healing in my body.

God is taking care of me. But here's the strange part—he's done much of it without my awareness. Not that God was working so secretly; the truth of the matter is that he has faithfully been working in my life even when I have disregarded him or felt aloof towards him.

However, let me be clear about this: God has not taken care of me so splendidly because I have been a super Christian. I haven't. In fact, sometimes I can relate to Paul when he refers to himself as the "chief of sinners." God has taken care of me because he loves me and he initiated that love even before I knew him. What a tragedy to take all of this for granted by failing to trust him with my future. What a ridicule of God's love to scorn his past care by putting my trust in other things.

As I reflect on my heritage, I would conclude that God has been taking care of me even before I was born. During World War II, my father worked at an airbase as part of the British Commonwealth Air Training Program. He didn't serve overseas but he repaired the fuselages of damaged bombers and fighter planes that had been shipped back to Canada during the course of the war. One day, when the bomb bay of a plane was opened as part of a regular repair procedure, an errant bomb dropped a fair distance to the pavement, right at his feet. The bomb did not detonate. In that gloomy hangar in the middle of the Canadian prairies, God protected my father from harm.

As well, when my mother was a little girl, she experienced her own daunting brush with death. At the age of three, she contracted rheumatic fever and became very sick. At her lowest point, the family was gathered around her bed, watching her gasp her last breaths. Judging by all apparent signs, her family was ready to pronounce her dead when, all of a sudden, she began to breathe again and her heart started to beat. And it continued to beat for over 80 more years. Long before any of my sisters or my brother and I were a glint in my parents' eyes, God was orchestrating my survival and ordering the steps of my lineage.

But my story stretches back at least one generation further. In the spring of 1912, the greatest ocean liner of its day was set to be launched from Great Britain. Dubbed unsinkable, the Titanic was about to sail her maiden voyage. Over 2,000 fortunate passengers had tickets to experience this historic event; among those passengers were two British citizens by the names of Edgar and Gertrude Olney—my grandparents.

You know how the story goes, but what you wouldn't know is that a few days before the great vessel set sail, my grandmother had an uneasy feeling about traveling on that particular ship. She suggested to my grandpa that they cash in their tickets and take a different boat. My grandfather was a very stern Englishman who was unaccustomed to taking orders or even suggestions from his wife. But on this occasion, his heart was soft, and he listened to the voice of my grandmother who, inadvertently, saved their lives. Their social standing would have relegated them to the steerage levels, where very few passengers were able to escape.

So, for at least 100 years, and probably even more, God has been taking care of me. In fact, the first chapter of Ephesians says God has had me on his mind for a lot longer than that.

The Scriptures tell us that God is the only secure resting place for our trust. *"Trust in the Lord always, for the Lord God is the eternal Rock"* (Isaiah 26:4). That is the official and correct answer. Personally, as I think about how God has ordered my steps and preserved my life to this point, I have no other sensible conclusion but to trust him fully with every aspect of my being. He loves me more than I can ever understand, and all other sources of trust will one day fail. God seems to think he alone is worthy of our trust; there's an extremely good chance that he is right.

Chapter 23

"I like you more than you think."

"The Lord is like a father to his children, tender and compassionate to those who fear him. For he knows how weak we are; he remembers we are only dust."

~Psalm 103:13–14

Why do we picture God as being more angry than happy? Many Christians go through life believing God is disgusted with them. They picture him as a peeved father who has, once again, been let down by his incompetent children. Because we do not see ourselves as living up to his expectations, we conceive that he is perpetually disappointed with us. Though this image is hard to shake, if we truly thought like God we would realize that, as his children, he likes us more than we think.

Of course God loves me. But does he like me? Is there joy in his heart when he thinks of me? Many believers find it difficult to envision God being pleased with them. Sure, he forgives me and loves me because of the work of his Son on the cross, but does he truly like me?

Indeed, those who do not fear God, those who regard themselves as their own masters, and those who believe they need to live only by their own standards of righteousness are in trouble. Those who snub the sacrifice of God's Son and regard it as nothing put themselves in a very precarious situation. In the final judgment, God's love and compassion will go only as far as humans have welcomed it. Sinners who reject the Lord's salvation will experience his wrath in its full fury. But sinners who repent and follow Christ will be welcomed into his eternal glory as deeply cherished children.

As his children, we struggle to comprehend God's affection for us because we are very performance-minded. Our heads tell us God loves us but our hearts tell us we are not good enough. We tend to think of our relationship with him in legal terms. Because we continue to break his laws, he cannot like us that much. Now, there is value in caring about our level of obedience—I am not promoting a libertine perversion of the gospel (sinning more so grace increases)—but we are misrepresenting God if we think our relationship with him is to be based more on obeying laws than on love.

It is very dangerous when we become too familiar with Christian language. As we talk about the love of God repeatedly, it begins to sound cliché. God is love . . . yah, whatever. I've heard that one before. Isn't that part of his job description, to love the world? We become jaded and don't even think about the meaning of the words.

Typical family relationships afford us the same misunderstanding regarding parental love. What does a parent's love mean to the average teenager? Do they know Mom and/or Dad loves them? What does it mean for a child to hear parents say "I love you"? Yes, Mom and Dad love them, but sometimes adolescents want to know if their parents really like them.

There is a marked difference between loving and liking. Loving is more an unconditional act of the will. It can involve emotion but it is primarily a cerebral decision. Because they came from my very being and because they are my very flesh and blood, I love my children unconditionally. There is nothing they can do that will make me stop loving them. But liking is more emotional, more spontaneous, more playful. I love my children but I do not always like what they do. Occasionally, they upset me (as I do them). But generally speaking, I both love and like my kids. The question we are considering here is: Does God go beyond officially loving to a point where he is even emotional, spontaneous, and playful with his children?

There are several angles from which we can approach this question. Perhaps a chronological analysis will serve us best here. What was the nature of his relationship with the very first human? When God created Adam, we get the impression that he liked him. He wanted him to have enjoyable things: a lot of good food, some animals to play with, and a beautiful wife for companionship, help, and physical intimacy. As well, it seems he wanted to fellowship with his creation, as indicated by his walks in the garden in the cool of the day (Genesis 3:8). Even when Adam and Eve messed up, he provided a substitutionary sacrifice to atone for their sin (Genesis 3:21). From all appearances, God seems to have liked his first humans, even as they stumbled out of the blocks.

Other early biblical stories continue to paint a picture of God's affection for those who chose to follow him wholeheartedly. The story of Enoch tells of a man who was swept away by the Lord without dying because God enjoyed his presence so much. *"Enoch lived 365 years, walking in close fellowship with God. Then one day he disappeared, because God took him"* (Genesis 5:23–24). Abraham was called God's friend on several occasions (2 Chronicles 20:7, Isaiah 41:8, James 2:23). In the story of Moses, we see that God spoke personally to him, as one would to a friend (Exodus 33:11).

When God began to call out a nation for himself by establishing the children of Israel, it is very evident that he had fond affection for his chosen people. Moses wrote,

Of all the people on earth, the Lord your God has chosen you to be his own special treasure. The Lord did not set his heart on you and choose you because you were more numerous than other nations, for you were the smallest of all nations! Rather, it was simply that the Lord loves you, and he was keeping the oath he had sworn to your ancestors. (Deuteronomy 7:6–8)

Hosea wrote,

When Israel was a child, I loved him, and out of Egypt I called my son. But the more I called Israel, the further they went from me. They sacrificed to the Baals and they burned incense to images. It was I who taught Ephraim to walk, taking them by the arms; but they did not realize it was I who healed them. I led them with cords of human kindness, with ties of love; I lifted the yoke from their neck and bent down to feed them. (Hosea 11:1–4 NIV)

These are powerful images of intimacy.

Even when Israel behaved in a metaphorically adulterous manner, God could not stop loving her. "*My people are determined to turn from me . . . How can I give you up, Ephraim? How can I hand you over, Israel? . . . My heart is changed within me; all my compassion is aroused*" (Hosea 11:7–8). The children of Israel did everything possible to tick God off, but he continued to relate to them from a position of love, even when he disciplined them.

As was discussed in chapter 5, when God gave Moses directions for the construction of the tabernacle and the ark of the covenant, he was also communicating something about his feelings for mankind.

You shall put the mercy seat on top of the ark, and in the ark you shall put the testimony which I will give to you. There I will meet with you; and from above the mercy seat, from between the two cherubim which are upon the ark of the testimony, I will speak to you about all that I

will give you in commandment for the sons of Israel.
(Exodus 25:21–22 NASB)

If we are going to think like God, we need to understand that his approach to humanity is always from a position of grace and mercy. If we are interested in walking in his ways, he is very tender with us.

The Psalmist reflected on the Lord's care for his children and concluded, *"How precious are your thoughts about me, O God. They cannot be numbered!"* (Psalm 139:17) And again, *"Many, O LORD my God, are the wonders which You have done, and Your thoughts toward us; There is none to compare with You. If I would declare and speak of them, they would be too numerous to count"* (Psalm 40:5 NASB). It appears as though God is thinking about me a lot. And, perhaps, these thoughts may be more positive than negative.

Let's jump ahead a few hundred years. When Jesus came to earth, he was friendly with people. Those who interacted with the Lord would have felt that he liked them. He referred to Lazarus as his friend (John 11:11). Interestingly, his spiritual enemies never called him a jerk; they referred to Jesus as a *"friend of tax-collectors and sinners"* because he went to parties in their houses (Matthew 11:19, Luke 7:34 NIV). Sinners felt that Jesus was a good friend.

So did his disciples if they were listening:

There is no greater love than to lay down one's life for one's friends. You are my friends if you do what I command. I no longer call you slaves, because a master doesn't confide in his slaves. Now you are my friends, since I have told you everything the Father told me. (John 15:13–15)

Jesus not only exemplified friendship, love, and compassion for his acquaintances throughout his earthly ministry, he taught us thoroughly regarding his Father's true feelings of kindness for mankind. He said that every sparrow in the world is under the watchful eye of his Father and that we, as his children, are far more valuable than a whole flock of birds. He said God tenderly cares for all plant life on this planet, adorning some members with immeasurable beauty. And yet, the Creator loves us far more than any plant with its incredibly short lifespan (Luke 12).

When Jesus wanted to tell us what his Father thinks of us wayward sinners, he told the story of the prodigal son (Luke 15). There is nothing in this story that warranted the father liking the son. Quite frankly, the boy was a big jerk. He stubbornly ignored his solid upbringing, made a rash and foolish decision, snubbed his father to his face, and proceeded to waste half of the value of his dad's estate, which had been built over many years of sacrifice and hard work. But the story seems to indicate that the father (God) looked daily for the son, in hopes that he would return to discover how much Dad still liked him, how much Dad still wanted to eat a good meal together with him.

Beyond just loving his wayward son, the father in this story wanted to show him how much he liked him. He wanted him to be decorated in jewellery and fine clothing and wanted to have a public feast, where all the neighbors could see how much the father liked his boy.

Why can't we see this level of warmth and affection in our own relationship with God? Why do we continue to believe he is not really fond of us? Let's get this straight—he is thinking about us. He is patiently waiting for us to discover the things we need to learn in life. He is pleased with our gestures of praise, worship, and prayer. He is happy that we took time out of our day to think of him. Most people didn't. He delights in the fact that we prayed to him for two minutes; he is not angry that we didn't pray for four. On occasion, he may even brag to the devil about how proud he is of one of his children in particular (Job 1:8).

And it's only going to get better into the future: *"No eye has seen, no ear has heard, and no mind has imagined what God has prepared for those who love him"* (1 Corinthians 2:9).

As his children, we can't even imagine the spectacular things God has prepared for us in heaven. He says we've never seen anything like it; we've never heard anyone talk about it; in fact, no human brain can even conjure up imaginary images that could compare to the enjoyable things that God will give to his kids in the future—all because he really likes us.

Having said that, I must reiterate my earlier point about God's grace and who will receive it in the end. If you do not heed God or his Word, and if you do not cry out in repentance for the forgiveness of your sins, you are not safe; you should be afraid. No—you should be very afraid. God is not a blind, benevolent do-gooder, doling out eternal life indiscriminately, making everything all right for everybody in the end. Yes, God is patient, not wanting anyone to perish, desiring all to come to salvation. But make no mistake, there will be a horrible price to pay in the end for ignoring God.

On the other hand, to enter into a personal relationship with God through the atoning blood of Jesus puts us in a unique position. We become his sons and daughters. We have the ability to interact personally with the Creator of the universe. These words sound absurd, but they are true.

God desires to have a personal relationship with those who respond to his grace. As James says, *"Draw near to God and he will draw near to you"* (James 4:8 NASB). Intimacy with the Almighty? What a concept, what a challenge! It begins with a basic fear and respect for the Creator and then grows into a beautiful relationship, full of deep communication and inside interaction. Prayer is ongoing. Obedience becomes habitual. Consciences remain pure. The light of God warms our hearts instead of scaring us to hide in the dark.

God wants us to know him personally. *"He offers friendship to the godly"* (Proverbs 3:32). It truly can be that simple. We are the ones that complicate the relationship. We have wrong views of God, usually making him more of a negative person than positive. We are the ones that make him out to be too distant. We are the ones who stubbornly do our own thing. We are the ones who rebelliously choose to not trust him. When we do not feel like he is close, we are the ones who moved away.

If God had his way with us and we began to think more like him, he would want us to feel his pleasure through our obedience to his Word, to know his affectionate heart in every situation we experience, and to enjoy the new mercies that he creates for us every morning. When we are obedient children, there is no limit to the level of intimacy we may experience with God. The Scriptures are quite clear about this matter—he likes us more than we think.

Chapter 24

"Will it matter in 100 years?"

"Your life is like the morning fog—
it's here a little while, then it's gone."

~James 4:14

Every day we face a plethora of decisions. Will we buy or sell Apple stock? Will we have Cheerios or toast? Will it be the black or the brown Rossetti's? Will we speed on the way to work? Will we talk to that annoying person or ignore them? Will we stop working hard when the boss leaves the office? Will we play along with that co-worker who tends to flirt with us? Will we respectfully turn off our cell phones during the meeting, or will we text secretly under the table? Will we expend a great deal of energy worrying about something? Will we devote some quality time to our spouse and/or children before they go to bed? Will we take notice of God at least once during the day?

At every juncture of our day we face choices—some profound, some superficial. How do we judge whether or not what we are doing is profitable? How do we make the most of our lives so that our valuable time, energy, and resources are not completely wasted? What do we do with confusing alternatives? What does it mean to think like God when we

face a decision that is not obvious or mandated in the
Scriptures? Should I have an affair? That's a no-brainer. But
should I buy that new Lexus? Maybe.

Thomas Hobbes referred to mankind's natural lot in this life
as "solitary, poor, nasty, brutish, and short."[8] The suffering
saint Job said,

> How frail is humanity! How short is life, how full of
> trouble! We blossom like a flower and then wither. Like a
> passing shadow, we quickly disappear . . . You have decided
> the length of our lives. You know how many months we will
> live, and we are not given a minute longer. (Job 14:1–5)

The clock is running but there is a time limit. Eternity is right
around the corner. To human thought, it is perplexing that
such a short period of time determines a never-ending
outcome. How do we get it right in our little window of
opportunity?

Every once in a while, I imagine what people like me were
thinking about 100 years ago. What went through the minds of
our predecessors who lived a century before us, making their
way through their busy days, each with their own seemingly
important concerns, similar to ours today? What were their
hopes, dreams, and aspirations? As significant as their lives
would have seemed to them back then, I would venture to say
that not one of those people is physically alive today. My
question, then, is this: What did those people do with their
lives that matters today, 100 years later?

As Christians, we often talk about making decisions in
light of eternity. This is not necessarily helpful. As frail
humans with limited brain power, we have a hard time
wrapping our grey matter around the concept of eternal life (or
eternal death, for that matter). Our finite intelligence cannot
grasp infinity with even moderate comprehension nor can we

---

[8] Thomas Hobbes, *Leviathon* (1651). As viewed online at http://oregonstate.edu/
instruct/phl302/texts/hobbes/leviathan-c.html (accessed Nov. 21, 2008).

talk about it with lucidity. And so I fear that, because of busyness, our inability to visualize eternity, and the forces of worldliness pummeling us regularly, we end up living life day to day, with not much foresight regarding our infinite existence and the future significance of the decisions we make today.

Ah, but 100 years we can grasp. And asking the question "Will it matter in 100 years?" is basically the same as asking "Will it matter in eternity?" In both cases, our physical life is complete. Our eternal state has been determined. So I want you to think with me for a minute—what *will* matter in 100 years? If we spend some time on this task, we may just end up thinking a little bit more like God. And, perhaps, we may start to worry less about the things that don't matter.

We are born into this world with a host of latent talents and future potential. Time and maturity teach us that we all have so much to contribute to friendships, families, organizations, companies, and ultimately, the kingdom of God. As we grow up, we take increasing steps of independence and find our own way through life. At some point, we reach the plateau of being totally responsible for every decision we make. Every thought, every choice, every worry, and every action pieces together a story that is uniquely our own. Our tales are exciting, peppered with successes as well as failures, joys as well as disappointments.

Today, each of us stands on the threshold of the next chapter of our own narrative, a plotline that will continue to be told into the future in one form or another, even long after we are dead. What will be our stories in 100 years from now? What will be our legacies? What will have survived? And most importantly, where will we be? What will matter in 100 years?

We are fairly self-absorbed. We consider our issues and matters of concern to be imperative. We believe our anxieties must be settled promptly. Those of us on the compulsive side disburse large quantities of our vigor stressing about tiny stuff.

Imagine if we could total the time wasted on worry, especially worry about events that did not end up occurring. Imagine if we could total the time wasted on worry related to things that did happen but have no eternal significance. What's the point of all our stress?

It's unfortunate we don't exert as much effort on obedience as worry. Stressing over the wrong things may reflect that we do not actually believe in heaven. We say we believe in it but we don't act like we do—so then, what do we truly believe? We are overly focused on the here and now. The temporal becomes so important because, if we are honest with ourselves, we live like this is all there is. A financial portfolio heading into the toilet is just that; it is not a matter of eternal significance. Does it matter today that millions of middle class Germans lost their life's savings with the collapse of the mark in the early 1920's? Will it matter in eternity?

Of course, life going badly is annoying and frustrating to our emotions. But can we pull ourselves out of the fog in order to see a bigger picture? Saving seems to be a good principle in life, but how do we refrain from making the mistake of saving up the wrong things? Humanly, we want to enjoy the now, but can we draw near enough to the heart of God to hear the humming of heaven?

This world tries to educate us about what matters. It tells us glamorous legends of wealth and influence, of pleasures and early retirement plans. It tries to convince us that life is about us. This world pretends to fill our lives with meaning apart from God. It attempts to convince us that beer is more fun than Jesus and that recreational sex and drugs are harmless side shows.

As God allows us to write our stories, we need to be committed to spotting the deceptions that will derail us and make a waste of our time on earth. How tragic for those who are oblivious to the devastation of a life of sin—her paycheck is massively destructive. Just ask young crystal meth addicts who now realize they will, most likely, never realize the full potential of the dreams of their youth, nor can they see their way clear to a hopeful future in heaven—all because for one split second they believed one of the devil's many lies.

So, beware; we write our stories in the midst of a battle, a spiritual battle for our souls and the souls of our loved ones. Spiritual forces of darkness want us to maintain our tunnel vision on the immediate and the useless. Demons want us to fret about the colors in our family room clashing rather than remember we are one day closer to eternity.

But here's the good news: our stories can be a success. We can get it right. In 100 years, our stories can be ones that glitter like gold. Our stories do not need to be ones ravished by worldliness and total failure.

Yes, there are songs to be written and inventions to be created. There are games to be played and books to be crafted. There are fortunes to be made and lovers to be wed. There are houses to be built and children to be raised. But the sooner we figure out what life is really about, the better. As Rick Warren so aptly reminds us, life is not about us.[9] True life is about following Jesus and seeing everything we do as a potential to serve him and his kingdom—the kingdom of God.

And here is a little tip: creating a meaningful legacy that will last 100 years and beyond comes more through an accumulation of many little deeds than through some single great accomplishment. It is our steady faithfulness in the small things that matters; this is what creates a long-lasting, beautiful story. Our attention to honesty, to godliness, to holiness, to allowing the Spirit of God to work in our lives—these are the things that matter.

Our faithful attention to serving other people, especially the needy, and to prayer and spiritual nurturing from the Scriptures—these are the things that will write a great story far into eternity. These low-profile items are like the small rudder that properly directs the big ship of our lives to a place of eternal significance, to do great things for God, and to

---

[9] Rick Warren, *The Purpose Driven Life* (Grand Rapids, MI: Zondervan, 2002).

influence people for good. Oftentimes, these good decisions are made quietly and unassumingly. Sometimes God is the only one who knows right now how great a life has been. But in time, it will be revealed to all.

The Bible tells an interesting life story of the prophet Daniel. When Daniel was a young man, he became a prisoner of war, taken from his home country and dragged off to a foreign land where he was forced to write quite a different story than what he probably dreamed of as a little lad. But in this foreign, pagan land, Daniel was faithful in the little things that matter and God made quite a lasting chronicle of his life. My favorite part of his biography is recorded in Daniel 6.

> *Darius the Mede decided to divide the kingdom into 120 provinces, and he appointed a high officer to rule over each province. The king also chose Daniel and two others as administrators to supervise the high officers and protect the king's interests. Daniel soon proved himself more capable than all the other administrators and high officers. Because of Daniel's great ability, the king made plans to place him over the entire empire. Then the other administrators and high officers began searching for some fault in the way Daniel was handling government affairs, but they couldn't find anything to criticize or condemn. He was faithful, always responsible, and completely trustworthy.* (Daniel 6:1–4)

As we continue to read the account, we see that Daniel's jealous colleagues cooked up a scheme that involved tricking the king into signing a goofy law declaring it illegal for the next 30 days to pray to anybody but the king. Violators of the law were to be eaten by lions. Notice Daniel's decision in response to this:

> *But when Daniel learned that the law had been signed, he went home and knelt down as usual in his upstairs room, with its windows open toward Jerusalem. He prayed three times a day, just as he had always done, giving thanks to his God.* (Daniel 6:10)

If you don't know how the story ends, read the rest of the chapter for yourself. But the true impact of the account lies in the remarkable words used to describe Daniel: "faithful, always responsible, completely trustworthy, as usual, windows open, praying, just as he had always done." These good habits of mind and behavior, these consistencies, made Daniel into a great man of God, a man whose life counted 100 years later and beyond.

As a good friend of mine used to say, "Every day you get to decide who you're going to be." We have not yet finished turning out. As we proceed from this day forward, we still have a lot of decisions to make. On an ongoing basis, we need to choose how to behave appropriately in the area of our sexuality. We need to decide whether or not we will forgive someone who has hurt us profoundly. We may opt for a career change that will open the door to a wider and more meaningful impact on the world at large. Every new day we choose how we are going to treat our spouses, children, neighbors, friends, and fellow-workers.

We need to decide how much to tithe, giving of our income back to God. We need to make up our mind on how to become involved in our local church and how many starving children in third world countries to sponsor. We need to settle on what to do with the poor, the homeless, and the needy in our neighborhoods as well as how we are going to love and serve our fellow man.

And as we do all these things wisely, we are making choices that will matter in 100 years. Either God's kingdom will be advanced or our own little kingdoms will be temporarily enhanced. But you see, the key word is "temporarily," because our little kingdoms will one day quickly crumble and only what is done for Jesus Christ will have indestructible significance and eternal reward.

Our Savior said those exact words to Martha when she was excessively concerned about creating the perfect dinner party while her sister sat at Jesus' feet, listening to his words.

But the Lord said to her, "My dear Martha, you are worried and upset over all these details! There is only one thing worth being concerned about. Mary has discovered it, and it will not be taken away from her." (Luke 10:41–42)

But a secure future in 100 years as well as into eternity goes beyond merely being near Jesus and hanging out with his people. Personal obedience and refraining from evil seem to be key ingredients.

Work hard to enter the narrow door to God's Kingdom, for many will try to enter but will fail. When the master of the house has locked the door, it will be too late. You will stand outside knocking and pleading, "Lord, open the door for us!" But he will reply, "I don't know you or where you come from." Then you will say, "But we ate and drank with you, and you taught in our streets." And he will reply, "I tell you, I don't know you or where you come from. Get away from me, all you who do evil." (Luke 13:24–27)

As a school administrator, I often find myself dealing with students making, or about to make, poor choices. To help them see the bigger picture associated with their choice, I encourage them to "finish the story." What I mean by this is to talk through the events that will likely transpire if they pursue their present course. Where will those actions or attitudes take them? Is that where they want to be? What other choices could be made to take them to where they want to be?

Finish the story of your life right now. Where do you want to be in 100 years? In eternity? What choices will get you to where you want to be at that time? What choices don't really impact this most vital issue? What should be considered peripheral?

A personal paradigm that involves "finishing the story" and "what matters in 100 years" is very powerful. It can alleviate a lot of pressure. Sincere believers can worry themselves sick about making a mistake, picking the wrong direction, and missing God's will for their life. It does not need to be that complicated. As we discussed in chapter two: fear God so that we don't have to fear anything else. Avoid obvious evil, and as you pour over your various options of choice, just ask yourself—what will matter in 100 years?

When facing a choice, sometimes different options can all be within the will of God as long as we are pursuing God in the midst of the choice. The will of God is certainly more behavioral than geographical. Attitude, heart, and obedience affect the long term impact. What are we doing, and why? Often only we and God know the answer to that.

The story line that will be great and lasting in 100 years is the story that is built on the life and teachings of Jesus Christ. At the same time, I am not encouraging us to be timid or tentative about having aggressive goals and lofty dreams for our lives here on earth. We need to go ahead and write those great stories, keeping Jesus at the center of them. Let's build our houses and our companies; let's make outstanding contributions to the realms of art and academia; run with that grand idea that will blow Microsoft or Google right out of the water; and create those fabulous family memories. . . . But as we write our stories and face our challenges of choice, we need to ask ourselves always, every day of our lives—will it matter in 100 years?

Chapter 25

"My day will come."

*"The day of the Lord is near,
the day when destruction comes from the Almighty.
How terrible that day will be!"*

~Joel 1:15

How many times have puny humans shook their fists at God in defiance, mockery, or anger, casting aspersions on his character because the Almighty didn't come through for them the way they wanted or because it just felt good to yell at God? Because we think we don't see him in action that much, we mistakenly presume that perhaps we can get away with doing our own thing after all. As Solomon said, *"When a crime is not punished quickly, people feel it is safe to do wrong"* (Ecclesiastes 8:11). Maybe God does not know, nor care, nor even exist.

Reality check—God is very much alive, in charge, and not asleep at the wheel. He is not oblivious to mankind's ruination of his creation. One day, all will stand before him; one day, all things will be made right and true justice will prevail. He will have the last word, not because he is petty or stubborn, but because he had the first word. No matter what the present circumstances may lead us to believe, God is warning us: "My day will come."

When Jesus ascended into heaven after his resurrection, the angels told his disciples, *"Why are you standing here staring into heaven? Jesus has been taken from you into heaven, but someday he will return from heaven in the same way you saw him go!"* (Acts 1:11). The day of the Lord involves the second coming of Christ, but it is a far more cataclysmic event than what Christians have traditionally thought it to be.

The earliest scriptural references to this theme are found in the minor prophets:

The day is near when I, the Lord, will judge all godless nations! As you have done to Israel, so it will be done to you. All your evil deeds will fall back on your own heads. (Obadiah 15)

Sound the alarm in Jerusalem! Raise the battle cry on my holy mountain! Let everyone tremble in fear because the day of the Lord is upon us. It is a day of darkness and gloom, day of thick clouds and deep blackness. Suddenly, like dawn spreading across the mountains, a great and mighty army appears. Nothing like it has been seen before or will ever be seen again. (Joel 2:1–2)

And I will cause wonders in the heavens and on the earth— blood and fire and columns of smoke. The sun will become dark, and the moon will turn blood red before that great and terrible day of the Lord arrives. But everyone who calls on the name of the Lord will be saved, for some on Mount Zion in Jerusalem will escape, just as the Lord has said. These will be among the survivors whom the Lord has called. (Joel 2:30–32)

What sorrow awaits you who say, "If only the day of the Lord were here!" You have no idea what you are wishing for. That day will bring darkness, not light. In that day you will be like a man who runs from a lion—only to meet a bear. Escaping from the bear, he leans his hand against a

*wall in his house—and he's bitten by a snake. Yes, the day
of the Lord will be dark and hopeless, without a ray of joy
or hope.* (Amos 5:18–20)

The message rings throughout the major prophets as well:

*For see, the day of the Lord is coming—the terrible day of
his fury and fierce anger. The land will be made desolate,
and all the sinners destroyed with it.* (Isaiah 13:9)

And again,

*For the terrible day is almost here—the day of the Lord! It
is a day of clouds and gloom, a day of despair for the
nations.* (Ezekiel 30:3)

From the earliest revelations of God to man, the day of the
Lord was always presented as imminent. Studying the Old
Testament descriptions and allusions to this topic as a whole
reveals that the day of the Lord is a two-pronged affair,
involving punishment for the wicked on earth and salvation
for the righteous people of faith.

Many local catastrophes, invasions, and other natural
calamites in the biblical narratives are spoken of as part of the
day of the Lord, somewhat like a foreshadowing of the main
event still to come in the future. But chronologically, the last
Old Testament prophet referred to God's day as something
still to come in the future:

*The Lord of Heaven's Armies says, "The day of judgment is
coming, burning like a furnace. On that day the arrogant
and the wicked will be burned up like straw. They will be
consumed—roots, branches, and all."* (Malachi 4:1)

New Testament writers also spoke regularly of this
enormous event to come in the timeline of human history. Jesus
referred to it as *"the day"* (Luke 17:30) and *"the coming of the
Son of Man"* (Matthew 24). Paul called it the *"day of the Lord"*

(2 Thessalonians 2:1–3) and the *"day of Christ"* (Philippians 1:9–10). Peter called it the *"day of God"* (2 Peter 3:12), the *"day of the Lord"* (2 Peter 3:10), and the *"day of visitation"* (1 Peter 2:12). And John, author of Revelation, referred to it as the *"great day of their wrath"* (Revelation 6:17) and the *"great day of God almighty"* (Revelation 16:14).[10]

Regardless of what they called it, biblical writers all agree that there will come a time when God will, once and for all, settle the score, revealing to the world his sovereign power and righteous justice. Everyone will be accountable for what they have done. Evil deeds done in the dark will be brought into the light. Good deeds done in secret will be displayed for all to see. Persecuted believers from all times will be vindicated and put on display as being part of the winning team. Through both salvation and judgment, God will be glorified.

Part of thinking like God involves understanding and believing that, one day, he will have his day. Even though he appears to be silent for a while, he will get very visibly active again. All through time, righteous followers of the Lord have cried out repeatedly to God to hurry up and judge the wicked.

O Lord, the God of vengeance, O God of vengeance, let your glorious justice shine forth! Arise, O judge of the earth. Give the proud what they deserve. How long, O Lord? How long will the wicked be allowed to gloat? How long will they speak with arrogance? How long will these evil people boast? They crush your people, Lord, hurting those you claim as your own. They kill widows and foreigners and murder orphans. "The Lord isn't looking," they say, "and besides, the God of Israel doesn't care." (Psalm 94:1–7)

Certain events in history have prefigured this day and all that it entails. During the Exodus, God visited the Egyptians with some nasty judgments in the process of delivering his

---

[10] All phrases quoted in this paragraph are from the NASB translation.

people out of bondage. Jericho was destroyed while Rahab and her family were saved. Sodom and Gomorrah were burnt to a crisp while Lot and his family were delivered. And on several occasions, the divided kingdoms of Israel and Judah experienced severe judgments for their disobedience, although always with a remnant kept alive as a demonstration of God's mercy.

In each of these episodes, after a period of perceived absence from the scene, God showed up with two things on his mind: save those who are his and punish the wicked for their evil deeds. It has happened over and over as a perpetual preview, but as I said, the main event is still to come. It could start tomorrow, in a year, in ten years. No one knows but the Father, not even Jesus himself (Mark 13:32). Regardless, we need to be ready for it (Luke 12:36–48), even though most of the world will be partying or going about their usual affairs in total oblivion to their impending doom (Luke 17:22–37).

There have been many great days in history—Independence Day, Emancipation Day, Armistice Day, D-Day, VE-Day. Many famous men have had their day—Alexander the Great, Julius Caesar, Genghis Khan, Hitler, Stalin. Powerful organizations have had their day—the Catholic Church, the Roman Empire, the IMF, the US military, Hollywood.

But we need to know that we ain't seen nothin' yet. There has not been anything like the day of the Lord (Joel 2:2). Powerful men and organizations may have thought they were pretty hot stuff. They may have perceived themselves to be something special or may have convinced themselves that they had the authority to impact nations and control their own destiny. But no one has accomplished anything on this planet except by the permissive will of God. And the great day of reckoning is approaching, when all will be accountable for the opportunities and authority afforded them by the Almighty.

On that day, it will become clear that men have not been running the world after all. And on that day, it will not matter how wealthy, witty, or worldly powerful we are; all that will matter is which category we fall into—the wicked, who must endure the wrath of God in the Great Tribulation and the eternal punishment of hell, or the righteous, who are saved from God's wrath and brought up to heaven at the beginning of the day of the Lord (Revelation 7:9–17).

For those in the second category, Paul talks about their salvation this way:

We tell you this directly from the Lord: We who are still living when the Lord returns will not meet him ahead of those who have died. For the Lord himself will come down from heaven with a commanding shout, with the voice of the archangel, and with the trumpet call of God. First, the Christians who have died will rise from their graves. Then, together with them, we who are still alive and remain on the earth will be caught up in the clouds to meet the Lord in the air. Then we will be with the Lord forever. (1 Thessalonians 4:15–17)

But for those in the first category, the event will look quite different. From the view of an unsuspecting non-believer, this is what the day of the Lord will look like:

I watched as the Lamb broke the sixth seal, and there was a great earthquake. The sun became as dark as black cloth, and the moon became as red as blood. Then the stars of the sky fell to the earth like green figs falling from a tree shaken by a strong wind. The sky was rolled up like a scroll, and all of the mountains and islands were moved from their places. Then everyone–the kings of the earth, the rulers, the generals, the wealthy, the powerful, and every slave and free person–all hid themselves in the caves and among the rocks of the mountains. And they cried to the mountains and the rocks, "Fall on us and hide us from the face of the one who sits on the throne and from the wrath of the Lamb. For the great day of their wrath has come, and who is able to survive?" (Revelation 6:12–17)

What a contrast between these two different perspectives of the same event!

But until that day arrives, mockers will persist in saying that such a judgment is improbable because God hasn't shown up for so long. Peter talked about this attitude in his second epistle:

> *Most importantly, I want to remind you that in the last days scoffers will come, mocking the truth and following their own desires. They will say, "What happened to the promise that Jesus is coming again? From before the times of our ancestors, everything has remained the same since the world was first created."* (2 Peter 3:3–4)

Later in the same passage, Peter explains what is truly going on in the mind of God during this supposed "delay":

> *But you must not forget this one thing, dear friends: A day is like a thousand years to the Lord, and a thousand years is like a day. The Lord isn't really being slow about his promise, as some people think. No, he is being patient for your sake. He does not want anyone to be destroyed, but wants everyone to repent. But the day of the Lord will come as unexpectedly as a thief. Then the heavens will pass away with a terrible noise, and the very elements themselves will disappear in fire, and the earth and everything on it will be found to deserve judgment.* (2 Peter 3:8–10)

Predicting exact world events is impossible. Who knows what will happen next—more terrorist attacks, world wars, complete financial obliteration, severe global warming? We can make intelligent guesses and forecast likely scenarios based on our knowledge of past history, but we can never know for sure. However, this we do know for sure: Jesus Christ is coming back to save his faithful followers from the wrath of God that is about to be poured out on this wicked world. And this salvation comes through faith in God and obedience to his Word. Those who know him personally will not be overtaken by this dreadful affair because they are in the know. It's often said, "It's not what you know; it's who you know." Knowing God personally through Jesus and his sacrifice for our sins places us in a position of awareness and safety regarding this frightful event.

Paul describes it clearly for us:

> *For you know quite well that the day of the Lord's return will come unexpectedly, like a thief in the night. When people are saying, "Everything is peaceful and secure," then disaster will fall on them as suddenly as a pregnant woman's labor pains begin. And there will be no escape. But you aren't in the dark about these things, dear brothers and sisters, and you won't be surprised when the day of the Lord comes like a thief. For you are all children of the light and of the day; we don't belong to darkness and night. So be on your guard, not asleep like the others. Stay alert and be clearheaded. Night is the time when people sleep and drinkers get drunk. But let us who live in the light be clearheaded, protected by the armor of faith and love, and wearing as our helmet the confidence of our salvation. For God chose to save us through our Lord Jesus Christ, not to pour out his anger on us. Christ died for us so that, whether we are dead or alive when he returns, we can live with him forever.* (1 Thessalonians 5:2–10)

Thinking like God involves many aspects, but none more important than this facet here. God's day will come. He knows it; his followers know it. Those who don't know the Lord, nor care, will, on that day, wish they had. One day, every knee will bow, voluntarily or by force. There are no words to describe the folly—no, stupidity—of rejecting the love, mercy, and forgiveness of God offered now while there is yet time.

It matters not how many of us believe it, the truth is still the truth. Don't be fooled—God is telling us, "My day will come."

Conclusion

The premise of this book is that we do not naturally think like God, which hinders us from living properly in this world and disqualifies us from an eternity with him in heaven. The good news is that there is hope; we can recover from this intellectual and spiritual handicap.

We can learn to think like God by listening carefully to what he says and making a concerted effort to close the gap between divine and human thought. As we make that effort, God will renovate us into something better. *"Let God transform you into a new person by changing the way you think"* (Romans 12:2).

Our natural thinking is tiny, earthly, arrogant, and presumptuous. If we fail to change our faulty ideas, human desires will always be too prominent in our decision-making and God will be relegated to a genie or doorman deity. Without tuning in to his thought patterns, we stay chained to the tease of temporal enchantments, wallowing in the muck of worldliness and sin.

Some books appear to be written to bring God closer to man. This book has been written to try to bring man closer to God. Let's not bring him down to make him more human; let's pursue an upward path that takes us closer to the divine through the blood of Jesus and an overhaul of our thought paradigm. After all, we were created in his image, not he in ours.

I believe he once inspired the phrase, *"Be imitators of God"* (Ephesians 5:1 NASB). When we have children of our own, the maturation goal is for them to think more like us, not vice versa. As his dear children, we need to mimic him. And the best way to mimic someone is to learn how they think. Actors playing character roles do it all the time. It works.

However, learning to think like God is not a simple task. The process, and it is a process indeed, takes humility and submission. It requires a lot of dying to self. It is often painful because our sinful nature does not want to go down easily. God graciously puts us through trials that human thinking cannot handle. He disciplines us so that we will reach out to him for divine perspective. If we seek after him, he gives us what we need—the harsh and the sublime—so that we can be transformed into someone better, a new creature.

And as we press on with this challenging journey, we can always look to our Savior as the author and finisher of our faith to help us along.

> *Since Jesus went through everything you're going through and more, learn to think like him. Think of your sufferings as a weaning from that old sinful habit of always expecting to get your own way. Then you'll be able to live out your days free to pursue what God wants instead of being tyrannized by what you want.* (1 Peter 4:1–2 MSG).

What a fabulous promise: to walk in the freedom of harmony with God—free from our lusts, free from selfishness, and free to be all we were created to be, both now and for eternity!